D1589266

JUDY BLAME'S OBITUARY
Writings on Fashion and Death

Derek McCormack is a writer who lives in Toronto. His recent books include 'The Well-Dressed Wound' and 'Castle Faggot', both published by Semiotext(e).

JUDY BLAME'S OBITUARY
Writings on Fashion and Death

Derek McCormack

Pilot Press

CONTENTS

AUTHOR'S NOTE

Fagginess is what I write about. I focus on things that fags
love: fashion and death. Think about it: all fags wear fashions
—I'm wearing some!—and all fags die—I'm dying! I started
out in fiction. I wrote novels about growing up gay. After a
couple of books came out, I began to get invitations to write
nonfiction. I wrote reminiscences about what it was like
writing novels about growing up gay. I interviewed gay artists
and writers. I did lots of fashion articles. Most of them date
back to my stint as a fashion columnist for the *National Post*, a
daily newspaper in Canada. The *Post* was politically
conservative; fortunately, the editorial board couldn't have
cared less about me. Thanks to my editor at the style section, I
got some great assignments: talking to famous fag designers
on their press tours through Toronto, travelling to New York
for fashion shows and fragrance launches. Vivienne
Westwood's office once offered a one-on-one interview with
her and I said no—I was too intimidated. I regret that. I regret
that I didn't propose profiles of other designers I admired,
Tom Binns, Rei Kawakubo and Andre Walker, in particular. I
was at the paper for five years or so; I cut out after doctors
discovered I had a rare and often fatal form of cancer. I'm still
alive. Sort of. I've continued to publish pieces here and there.
Lately I've contributed a couple fashion stories to *Artforum*—
my tribute to the late Judy Blame inspired the title of this
collection.

My tribute to Blame is about him and about me—there are lots of my own tales woven in with the topics I touch on. The articles here are a sort of autobiography, a life seen through a scrim, or a life as a scrim—my moire *mémoires*.

Derek McCormack

PETERBOROUGH

What's fun about a funhouse?

Fuck all.

When I was young, I'd go to the Peterborough Exhibition—I'd go in the haunted house and the funhouse.

The funhouse had a mirror maze. The maze wasn't all mirrors: there were mirrors and panes of plain glass. I'd stumble through it, smashing into glass, seeing my mirror selves smashing into glass.

The crowd on the midway looked and laughed.

Why did I do it?

Why not? The laughter didn't deter me. I grew up in Peterborough, a small city in Canada—I was used to getting laughed at.

When I walked down the street, I got laughed at. When I went to school, I got laughed at. Strangers called me a faggot. Students called me a faggot. Teachers called me a faggot. I got my head smashed into walls so many times, the city seemed to spin.

I didn't dare go to the Ex after dark. I'd be dead.

The school, the city—it all seemed to me to be a funhouse. I was its cartoon mascot—a fag with a scrawny body and feet as big as clown shoes. It was as if I'd emerged from a laughing mirror—that's what carnies call funhouse mirrors that are rippled to create comical reflections.

When I looked in a laughing mirror, it laughed at me.

Peterborough is a cruel place.

I fled it before finishing high school. I didn't move that far away. I went to Toronto and started writing. I started writing about Peterborough.

The first book of stories I published, *Dark Rides*, was set in Peterborough in the 1950s. It was set in and around the Peterborough Ex.

The central character was a fag named Derek.

He was beaten.

He was abused.

Wish Book, my second book of stories, was set in Peter—borough during the Depression. It, too, is set at the Ex. It, too, is full of fags being beaten and abused.

The stories starred the streets and stores I remembered. There was William Lech & Sons Furs and the stuffed black bear that for decades stood outside of it. Vandals tore off its ear. Vandals carved their names in its carcass. There was the Fun House, a joke shop with X-rated jokes—dick warmers, dick rulers. It sold magic tricks, too, and pranks. A bedbug made of metal. A soap that lathered up into black foam.

There was the Brock Ballroom, the concert hall at the centre of town. Hank Williams played there—he staggered onstage, started singing, then collapsed. It was the drugs, the booze, the back pain. It was Peterborough.

The Haunted Hillbilly, my first novel, was about Hank Williams.

It was set in Nashville, where a faggot vampire couturier takes control of Hank's career, steering him to stardom, then to ruin.

The vampire narrates the novel in the first person.

The vampire is me.

While the book is supposedly set in Nashville, it's really set in Peterborough. I moved some Nashville landmarks to my hometown. The Brock Ballroom became the Ryman Auditorium; the Pig's Ear, Tootsie's Orchid Lounge.

The Ex turned into the Tennessee State Fair, where the vampire narrator vows to turn Hank into a kewpie doll—a glittery, gaudy piece of garbage.

Why do this? Peterborough is for me a sinister place, and the novel needed a sinister atmosphere. It also freed me for the first time to imagine Peterborough as it is in my dreams—a city of busy streets and back alleys, a city with questionable quarters and stylish stores. I imagined a carny district, where midway workers wintered in flop hotels. I imagined a wax district, where waxworks churned out statues for the museums that country stars erected in their own names. I imagined a gay district ringed by funeral homes—for all the fags who were murdered, or who murdered themselves.

You think Peterborough doesn't kill? Walk through Little Lake Cemetery.

It's full.

The Show That Smells, my second novel, was set entirely in a midway mirror maze.

What I'm trying to say is this: I didn't get out of Peterborough.

I built Peterborough in my books. I built it because it disgusted me, and I disgusted it, and the disgust I felt drove me to write.

When I hear writers talk about writing as freedom, as an expression of emotions, as a calling or a communication or a conversation, I laugh. I can't conceive of writing without disgust as the driving force—and as the desired effect.

Writing is devotion to disgust.

Am I cruel? Is it cruel to call a whole city cruel? Yes. I picked it up in my childhood. I have always wanted to give Peterborough back some of the pain it brought to me. So I think of my writing as a prank, the kind of prank I'd buy at the Fun House as a kid. This essay? It looks like a bedbug. This essay? It's a bar of soap. It's secretly made of ink.

2016

THE DIRT ON DRACULA

When I was a young faggot, I dreamed of being Dracula. I had the shit.

At Halloween, stores sold a Dracula cereal—Count Chocula—that tasted like chocolate. It made my shit brown— or browner, I should say.

What did my shit smell like? It smelled like the Count.

I had a Dracula air freshener. It looked like him—a wax vamp with black hair. Fangs. Drugstores stocked it at Halloween. A label on it said: "NOT TO BE EATEN."

Dracula killed people by eating them; he killed them, too, when they ate him.

The Dracula freshener said a lot about the Count. It spoke to his fame. It spoke to his association with Halloween. The Dracula air freshener was decor and deodorizer—it perched on the toilet tank, staring at me as I shat.

Dracula: like all fags, he was a pervert; like all fags, he hung around in bathrooms; like all fags, he wore perfume but the stink of shit still surrounded him.

At Halloween, I crept down the streets of my north-end neighbourhood, scheming to scare the shit out of kids. I had a cape. I had plastic fangs. I had fake blood on my fingers and chin. Some blood smeared onto my Sunday school suit, which was worrisome—fake blood doesn't always come out.

The kids weren't scared of me. They did what they always did: they called me a fucking fag. Vampire or fag—is there a difference?

"How dare you touch him, any of you?" Dracula hisses in *Dracula*, the book by Bram Stoker. He's hissing at the vampire hags who inhabit his castle. The hags have ganged up on Jonathan Harker, the Count's solicitor. The Count has a hissy fit. "How dare you cast eyes on him when I had forbidden it? Back, I tell you all! This man belongs to me!"

When I first read this, it filled me with want: I wanted Dracula to bite Jonathan, to drain him dry. It didn't happen. Stoker couldn't allow it. At that time, at the turn of the last century, there was something worse than being undead: being gay.

Bram Stoker was born in Dublin in 1847. He was bedridden for seven years by a disease that was never diagnosed.

Able at last to get out of bed, he went to a private school, then to Trinity College. As president of the Philosophical Society, he met Oscar Wilde. At Wilde's home, he met Florence

Balcombe, who was being wooed by Wilde. Stoker wooed and won her.

Stoker started writing *Dracula* in June of 1895. He conceived of an aristocrat, a strange aristocrat, a faggot of indecency and dread who betrayed no morality, but who betrayed morality, and who dreamed of spreading the disease of his Dracula-ness from Transylvania to England and throughout the world. Some say the germ for Dracula was Vlad the Impaler. It wasn't.

Wilde, the wit, the playwright, the world-famous teller of fairy tales—he was tried for gross indecency in a courtroom in London in May of 1895. Who wouldn't have convicted him? Wilde looked like an invert. He wore velvet suits. He wore green carnations in his suits. He wore a French perfume, Houbigant. The trial took three days. The evidence came and came. Detectives described the sheets from his bed: there was sweat on them. Sweat, semen and shit.

What does Dracula smell like? According to Stoker, it wasn't Houbigant: "But as to the odour itself, how shall I describe it? It was not alone that it was composed of all the ills of mortality and with the pungent, acrid smell of blood, but it seemed as though corruption had become itself corrupt. Faugh! it sickens me to think of it. Every breath exhaled by that monster seemed to have clung to the place and intensified its loathsomeness."

Dracula's the opposite of an air freshener: he's a de-freshener.

The Dracula air freshener I had was made by Wizard and worked by masking odours—it gave off scent until the scent wore off. Different air fresheners work in different ways. Air sanitizers deactivate bacteria. Adsorbent fresheners act like glue. Count Dracula, the character, was adsorbent: corruption clung to him.

Me? Fagginess clung to me.

What I wanted when I was young was to walk Peterborough and not feel afraid. The cure for fear, I thought, was inflicting fear on others. I found that as a vampire, I was a flop; as a fag, I was something else. I didn't scare people, but I could do other things: I could irk them; I could sicken them; I could even provoke them to the point of violence. In time I found that these powers pleased me. I was a vampire of some sort: I liked the taste of their distaste.

2019

THE MONSTER COMIC

I went to Nashville. I went to museums. Stars' museums. Barbara Mandrell had hers; Barbara Mandrell's Country, it was called. She exhibited the canes and crutches she used to recover from a car accident. Ferlin Husky had a museum with dioramas showing the life and death of Christ.

Wax museums. The city had lots. Greats behind glass. Whitey Ford. Jimmie Rodgers mid-yodel. Legend had it that Jim Reeves's widow visited the Country Music Wax Museum to comb his statue's hair.

I visited the Country Music Foundation and Hall of Fame on Music Row. I saw guitars and more guitars. I saw Stringbean's banjo.

"Where's the library?" I asked.

"Downstairs," the attendant said. Stairs led down to a gate to the basement. "Do you have an appointment?" The attendant said I needed an appointment and a referral from an archivist.

I left. What I really wanted were tapes, top-secret tapes. Nick Tosches mentions them in his 1977 book *Country*:

> The Country Music Foundation in Nashville possesses two interviews with promoter Oscar Davis…In his long and colorful career, Davis had worked intimately with Ernest Tubb, Hank Snow, Roy Acuff, Eddy Arnold, Hank Williams, Elvis Presley (whom Davis introduced to Colonel Tom Parker),

and hundreds more...He had nothing to lose, and he told it all: a great, glorious, scandalous *Who Fucked Who* of country music, full of homosexuality, pedophilia, and motel drunk-fucks. The CMF allows absolutely no access to these tapes.

I will never hear the tales on the tapes.
I decided to write them myself.

The Bible. Comic books. This is what Hank Williams read. He liked reading comic books. Jerry Rivers, who played with Hank's band, The Drifting Cowboys, once wrote:

> Jim Denny brought Hank back to Nashville where he went into Madison Hospital for rest and additional treatment for his previous back injury. After a few days, Don, Sammy, Cedric and I would drop by and see Hank in the evenings, bring him some of his favorite 'monster' comic books and laugh and joke about the road. But in the early mornings, Skip and I would sit on a damp wooded hillside, alone, and wonder if things would ever be like they were before. They never were.

Monster comics, aka horror comics, aka crime comics. EC published the most notorious titles: *Tales from the Crypt, Vault of Horror, Shocking SuspenStories.*

I have one of the first EC crime comics, *Haunt of Fear* from 1950. Hank Williams read it. Maybe. Probably. A man kills his wife, then her corpse attacks him. A mad magician tests his saw-a-body-in-half trick with a real saw and real bodies. A monster stalks a swamp. It's a blob of living matter. It smothers unsuspecting humans.

EC Comics sparked a crime comic craze. Comic companies across America churned them out. America and Canada. None captured EC's artistry. Superior Publishing in Toronto created some of the goriest scenes. Or so I've heard. I've never seen one. They're scarce.

They're illegal.

Clergy hated crime comics, as did teachers, parents and politicians. E.D. Fulton represented Kamloops in Canada's Federal Parliament. In 1949, he tabled a bill. Frederick Wertham testified on its behalf. Wertham, a psychologist from New York, crusader against crime comics in America. Wertham wrote:

> If later on you want to read a good novel it may describe how a young boy and girl sit together and watch the rain falling. They talk about themselves and the pages of the book describe what their innermost little thoughts are. This is what is called literature. But you will never be able to appreciate that if in comic-book fashion you expect that at any minute someone will appear and pitch both of them out of the window.

It passed. It still stands: the Fulton Bill, making it illegal for Canadians to write, sell or distribute "[t]he kind of magazine, forty or fifty pages of which portray nothing but scenes illustrating the commission of crimes of violence with every kind of horror that the mind of man can conceive."

Crime comics, Fulton argued, celebrated delinquency. Drug abuse. Pedophilia. Homosexuality.

Same stuff Oscar Davis let loose.

The Haunted Hillbilly is a crime comic. In words. I can't draw. A vampire story, à la *Dracula*. An ode to country's underside. My Mina Harker: a male country and western singer, an all-American boy. Cornfed. Clueless.

I named him Hank after Hank Williams. And Hank Snow, a Nova Scotian who dressed like a cowboy. And Hank Thompson, who made a hit of "The Wild Side of Life" in 1951.

My Renfield's a doctor. A gay doctor with a weakness for Hank's ass. Dr. Wertham, I called him.

Nudie's Dracula.

By day he runs a carnival. The haunted house kills. He sculpts wax statues for a sideshow wax museum. He tinsels kewpie dolls. He sews costumes for sideshow acts. Strong men. Spidoras: half-women, half-spiders. He's Nudie, the Carnival Couturier—the Thread Count.

By night, he's a ghoul. He becomes a bat. He commands an army of bats. He takes Hank under his wing, dressing him in suits with sequined skulls, sequined cobwebs, sequined bats. Sequins made from human bones. Bones he acquires from Hank's girlfriends.

Nudie's a spoof of several fashion figures. Nudie Cohn, the Rodeo Tailor, who designed the first rhinestone country ensemble. Another inspiration: country costumer Nathan Turk. Turk dressed Ernest Tubb in orange suits with black piping, black suits with orange piping. Ernest Tubb nicknamed his Turks. He had "Halloween," "Pumpkin," "Black Cat."

Turk shut his shop in 1977. He sewed Halloween costumes for his grandkids.

I went back to Nashville years later.

The Hall of Fame was gone, moved to a building on the banks of the Cumberland. A building shaped like a guitar.

Gone, too, were the stars' museums. Does nobody care about Barbara Mandrell anymore? Ferlin Husky's museum, Waylon Jennings's museum, Minnie Pearl's museum—gone. The Randy Travis museum. A candle shop leased the space.

The wax museums were gone, too. Downtown had died, tourists diverted to the Opryland theme park on the outskirts of town. In 1999, a reporter from *The Tennessean* went hunting for figures that had once filled the Country Music Wax Museum.

He found them in a basement beneath an office complex, bodies laid out like in a makeshift morgue. Bill Carlisle, limbs crooked as a corpse's. Minnie Pearl, hat on chest. The statues still dressed in clothes that stars and their families had donated. Jimmie Rodgers in one of Jimmie Rodgers' railroading suits. Carter Family in Sunday duds. The reporter spied a dozen ensembles by Nudie Cohn. A wig Barbara Mandrell designed for a Barbara Mandrell doppelgänger.

Not all the statues survived in such good shape. The reporter reported that Conway Twitty had been beheaded. Same with Stringbean. Someone stole Uncle Dave Macon's gold teeth. "And Hank Williams Jr. lay on his back with…a giant crack running along his neck." Vandals?

Vlad?

2004

MAISON MONSTER MARGIELA

I was watching *Buffy, the Vampire Slayer* on TV. I watch it religiously. The vampires were dressed in smart, slim suits.

I thought of other vampires. In the 1933 film *Dracula*, Bela Lugosi wears a plush cape. In "The Vampire," a story in *Tales from the Crypt*, the 1950s comic book, a vampire wears patent leather wingtips. Then turns into a bat.

Vampires dress dapper, I decided. But who makes their clothes?

I knew about vampires. As a kid I had a hand-puppet of The Count from *Sesame Street*. In grade three I went trick-or-treating in a rayon cape and wax fangs. The fangs were candy-flavoured. I ate them—or did they eat me?

I knew less about couture. I started reading *Vogue* and *Harper's Bazaar*. I haunted Holt Renfrew and other stores that sell upscale designs. What I saw was elegant, expensive. I wanted scary. Chanel's showing pastel half-capes. A vampire in a Chanel cape couldn't scare a fly. No vampire would wear Christian Lacroix.

Then one day I found myself in i-cii, a boutique in Yorkville that sells stuff by Martin Margiela, the Belgian designer. I tried on a shirt. It was two shirts, actually. Margiela had cut different shirts in half, then sewn mismatching halves together. The right side of my shirt was white. The left was cream. I had a square collar on one side, a spear collar on the other.

A shirt with a split personality. The perfect look, I thought, for Dr. Jekyll and Mr. Hyde.

Margiela keeps shop in Paris. He showed his first collection in 1988. He's never posed for a photograph. Never been interviewed face-to-face. *Vogue* recently photographed his atelier. He wasn't in the picture. An empty chair sat in his place.

His *maison* is in a derelict machine shop in a derelict arrondissement of Paris. It's tricked out like a lab. White walls. Chandeliers wrapped in white muslin. Margiela wears a white lab coat while he works. The press calls Margiela a "crazy professor." I prefer the B-movie term: mad scientist.

Margiela experiments with clothes like Dr. Frankenstein experimented with cadavers. His clothes aren't haute couture, but *haute horreur*. They're made for the living. They suit the undead.

COUTURE OF THE NIGHT

In 1988, a week before Halloween, Margiela staged his first show. In an abandoned theatre. Models wore boots that had been slathered in blood-red paint. The boots bloodied the catwalk. The models stumbled. Besides slippery soles, they had on eyeless black hoods. In a Margiela hood, it's always night. Skin's impervious to sun. For a model, it's disorienting. For a vampire, it's daywear.

NIGHTWEAR FOR NIGHTMARES

According to the book The *Language of Clothes,* female
phantoms "often...wear the classic white shroud, sometimes
stained with blood." A bloody shroud is de rigueur. It's the
little black dress of the ghost world. Margiela's done his
version of it. After his 1988 show, he cut up the cloth that
covered the catwalk. White cotton stained with red boot
prints. He sewed it into suits. He showed the suits with fake
white eyelashes. White-powdered hair. Even apparitions have
to accessorize.

TAILOR FROM THE CRYPT

Zombies are corpses who come back to life. Hair rotting. Suits
wormy. But zombie chic isn't just for cadavers. In 1997,
Margiela grew cultures: bacteria, yeast, and mold. He dyed
them yellow, green, and fuchsia. With a perfume atomizer he
spritzed them on suits and dresses. The clothes had been
coated with a mold-friendly medium. Care labels read: Don't
wash. The cultures grew. The dyes spread. The suits stank like
the grave.

WOLF IN CHIC CLOTHING

Margiela's wigs are swatches of fur cut from old coats. Mink, squirrel, weasel. On models they look like mullets. The models look like human-animal hybrids, the kind Dr. Moreau bred in *The Island of Dr. Moreau*. Moreau's monsters were part monkey, part man. Margiela doesn't make monkey rugs. Yet. Wolf wigs turn his models into werewolves. His other wigs turn them into less famous beasts: wereminks, weresquirrels, wereweasels.

FRANKENSATIN

Margiela's a grave digger of sorts. He finds materials for his clothes in second-hand stores, Salvation Army depots, abandoned warehouses. He rips up the clothes and remakes them. War surplus socks become sweaters. Silk suit linings become slips. Victor Frankenstein made a monster by stitching together dead body parts. Margiela's never sewn with skin. He did make a belt out of braided human hair. For the Fall 1995 show, his models put on pendant necklaces. The pendants were human ponytails. I don't know where he got those.

2001

BLANK BOOK

Ouija board? It's me, Derek McCormack. I was wondering: is
Martin Margiela a real man? Is there a chance he'd answer
some questions?

The Ouija board stays silent; the planchette does not stir. I
didn't think it would: the board is used to summon spirits,
and Martin Margiela—the Belgian fashion designer—isn't a
spirit. He only seems to be one.

It was worth a shot. I had a better chance of contacting a
ghost than of contacting Margiela. The man is renowned for
being unknown: after twenty years of fashion fame, he has not
granted a single interview, nor sat for a single photograph.
After his fashion shows, he does not take a bow.

Fans of Margiela's will find little information about him in
Maison Martin Margiela, a new monograph devoted to the
mysterious man. A beautiful object, bedecked with ribbon
bookmarks and detachable booklets, it bursts with photos of
his singular, signally great garb: wigs crafted from fur coats,
skirts sewn from the linings of old coats, vintage coats cut up
and reconfigured.

Margiela? There are no photos of him, no words from him.
He is as invisible as ever. Here in spirit only.

Is Martin Margiela real? The Ouija Board blanked me, but I
have heard things. I have heard that he is a woman; that his
clothes are designed by a collective; that he designed his line

up until the time that Diesel bought a majority stake in his *maison*. When I visit the Margiela store in New York City, I find myself asking the staff if he's been by. I don't know why I do. Margiela is a label whose clothes I've coveted. Man, woman, collective—the designer's identity doesn't affect the fit and fabrics. Why do I need to know about the man?

If he seems to be a spirit, I'm a spiritualist. I want to feel that he's real.

I learned of Margiela not long after he made his debut in 1989. He showed in Paris; Holt Renfrew brought his line into their store in downtown Toronto. Holt's staged a parade—female models dressed in Margiela shuffled through the store. The clothes were dark, blacks and blues. The clothes seemed incomplete, and inside-out: unfinished hems, exposed seams.

I did not fall for him. I was still in love with Jean Paul Gaultier. I had a couple pieces of Gaultier menswear: an orange jean jacket, a brown rubber shirt, a brooch that resembled a bobby's Brunswick star. I wore him when I wanted attention, which was all the time. I was studying philosophy at school, and my head was full of French theory, and French fashion. I had written an essay about Gaultier and Jean Baudrillard. Baudrillard believed that images had replaced reality; Gaultier was an image generator. From his French *maison*, he pelted the planet with his clothing, his perfume ads, his television show and his music videos.

I grew into Margiela. After abandoning school, I was hell-bent on being a writer. It became important to me that my books, and not my wardrobe, attract attention. Forget Baudrillard—I had taken to Roland Barthes, who argued that the author was dead. The text, he said, had the power to alter both writer and reader, to dissolve subjectivity; writing was what mattered. Margiela suddenly made sense to me. If I wore his clothes, I could be cool, but in a whispery way. The knowing would know what I was wearing; the unknowing would see me in deadstock, strange silhouettes, pieces seemingly picked from the Salvation Army store.

What does it mean to have a favourite designer? For me, it meant total devotion: I longed to disappear into Margiela's clothes, to turn into a whim of his—to be blanked by a blank. My personality? It was never that personable—erase it. My personal style? It was never that stylish—erase it. I'd seen instances of this erasure in literature. It was said that Maurice Blanchot, the French novelist and essayist, had never been photographed, never been interviewed face to face. For Georges Bataille, the act of undressing before sex induced a dissolution of selfhood; for me, the act of undressing in a changeroom had the same effect.

Margiela was a master of this vanishing act. The more he shunned the press and public, the more famous he became for doing so. He withdrew from the world and came back as a bogey. He seemed to spoof his own pose—he painted his *maison* all white, and shrouded furniture in white sheets. He covered his mannequins' faces with white masks. The photography in *Maison Martin Margiela* is reminiscent of spiritualist photography of the nineteenth century: models are mysterious blurs, shots are bleached by unseen lights, clothes droop from hangers like ectoplasm from mediums' mouths.

Why did I think that Margiela could work magic on me, could transform me into something and someone I was not? I have always idealized my idols. I ascribed occult powers to him, and longed for him to grant me supernatural style and substance. But he's no spirit. He's a talented designer who's played a terrific parlour trick: vanishing out of view, but haunting our heads.

2012

FRUIT BRUTE

When I was a kid, I watched the Wolfman. He was a character on my favourite Saturday morning tv show, *The Hilarious House of Frightenstein*. A venal vampire, a wacky witch—*Frightenstein* starred a cast of comical monsters. The Wolfman was a werewolf. An actor in a mask. He acted like Wolfman Jack.

The Wolfman deejayed. He'd play a record, something by the Rolling Stones, say, or the 1910 Fruitgum Company. Stepping in front of a green screen, he'd dance. Crazy colours whirled around him, shocking shades of red, yellow, green. The Wolfman was the world's first psychedelic werewolf. Seems to me that he inspired the world's second psychedelic werewolf, Fruit Brute.

I never ate Fruit Brute. I never will. It's not sold anymore. Fruit Brute was a breakfast cereal. General Mills made it in the 1970s. Mini-marshmallows mixed with lime-coloured lumps. The lumps didn't taste like lime. They tasted like sugar. The cereal's mascot was a werewolf, a cartoon character that looked a lot like the Wolfman I watched on tv. The Wolfman wore overalls. Fruit Brute wore overalls. Like the Wolfman, Fruit Brute loved colours—his overalls were striped with shocking shades of red, yellow, green. Smiley and silly, Fruit Brute was a flower-power werewolf, more hippie than horror.

33

Fruit Brute wasn't the first scary cereal. In the early 1970s, General Mills, maker of Cheerios and Wheaties, had an idea, a new way to sell its foodstuffs—horror. It came up with a couple of monster mascots. Count Chocula resembled Dracula. His cape—brown. Franken Berry spoofed the monster that Boris Karloff brought to life in the 1931 film *Frankenstein*. Karloff wore bolts in his neck. Franken Berry had bolts, too. And a steam pipe in his right temple. An alarm clock in his left. His steel eye sockets resembled spectacles. He looked like Elton John.

The cereals? Both were made of mini-marshmallows and skull-shaped corn pops. Count Chocula contained cocoa, or faux-cocoa. Franken Berry was strawberry. The dye didn't break down during digestion. Kids who ate it started shitting red. Parents mistook it for blood. Screamed. Did Count Chocula dye stools a different brown? Hard to tell. General Mills recalled its macabre breakfast cereals. It tried new dyes. When the cereals were rereleased, they sold out. It was Halloween.

What's the safest way to eat werewolf cereal? With a silver spoon. Cashing in on the success of its first monster cereals, General Mills released Fruit Brute in 1973. According to ads, Fruit Brute contained "the howling good taste of froooooot!" Boo Berry came out at the same time. Boo Berry was a ghost. But whose? Peter Lorre's, perhaps. There's a resemblance. A blueberry-flavoured breakfast cereal, Boo Berry made milk blue.

Boo Berry sold well. Fruit Brute did not. General Mills did its damnedest. It ran Fruit Brute spots during Saturday morning shows like *The Hilarious House of Frightenstein*. It tempted tots with a host of premiums. Some came included in the cereal boxes, like the Fruit Brute Glow Switchplate Cover, a decal that kids could lay over light switches. Some premiums required more work: kids had to mail away box tops, or box tops and money, too. Six to eight weeks later, they got a Magic Fruit Brute Puzzle, a plastic jigsaw game that glowed witch-green, or a colouring book called "How to be a Good Monster."

Halloween was prime premium time. General Mills offered plastic trick-or-treat bags printed with its monster mascots. Monster Disguise Kits included stickers shaped like eyebrows and scars. Kids slapped them onto skin. The priciest premiums: Fruit Brute costumes. Cut from cloth, the costumes came in one piece, slipping over trick-or-treaters' heads. They were square, silkscreened with the same graphics that the cereal boxes bore: "Artificial Flavor Frosted Cereal with Monster Mallows." Kids dressed up not as Fruit Brute, but as boxes of Fruit Brute. Stamped on their shoulders: "Provides 8 Essential Vitamins & Iron."

General Mills stopped making Fruit Brute in 1983. Four years later, they marketed the same cereal under a different name: "Fruity Yummy Mummy." Yummy Mummy proved as unpopular as its predecessor. It disappeared from store shelves. Dead again.

2005

HAIRY WINSTON

I walk into woods. A rutted trail. Stone-studded. It's spring. Wind's wintry. Branches black as riding crops.

In a clearing I come on carcasses. A couple of heads. Werewolf heads. They're huge. Big as small men. Dogs scamper around, snarling. A terrier tinier than a werewolf's tongue.

I inspect the decapitations. A snout's missing. A lower jaw gone. The heads look like they're decomposing. Skulls show. Crystals jut from them. Orange crystals. Phantom crystals in blues. White crystal needles called apophyllites.

David Altmejd did this. Altmejd's an artist. He studied sculpture in Montreal, his hometown, then moved to Manhattan. He's a star in the States. The Whitney Museum of American Art commissioned the sculptures and installed them in Central Park.

Altmejd had his first solo show in New York City in 2002. Days before Halloween. A full moon. The Hunter's Moon.

The show featured werewolves. He displayed them on pedestals and in mirrored vitrines. He dolled them up in crystals.

And cosmetics. Fur teased to the consistency of cobweb candy. Tongues spray-painted shocking pink. Some heads oozed what seemed to be cream. Night? Vanishing? I'm not sure. Do werewolves in night cream feel it's always night?

And cocktail jewelry. Skins sparkled with sequins and jewels. Provenance: Woolworth's. A stick pin stuck in a skull. A rhinestone brooch pierced a cheek. A bracelet of brilliants dangling from lips. Sculpted sparrows pecked at the bracelets as if bracelets were worms.

Eastern European werewolf lore. Sigmund Freud's Wolf Man case. Pagan rituals. Altmejd's sculptures suggested all of these. Mostly they hearkened to Hollywood. To *The Wolf Man*, a monster movie of 1941 that made werewolves a part of the popular psyche.

Lon Chaney Jr. plays Larry. A British count. With an American accent. Larry falls for Gwen. She clerks at an antique shop. When he meets her, she's trying on earrings. Sterling silver. Half-moons. He asks to buy them. She says they're not for sale. She should have sold—the next night Larry becomes a werewolf. He tracks Gwen across the moors. Attacks. I always wonder: Is he after her? Or her half-moons?

Altmejd feeds off this confusion. His werewolves hunger for bodies and for bijoux. Lycanthropes as Liberace.

His solo show was a smash. The Whitney invited Altmejd to show his sculptures in Central Park. And in this year's Whitney Biennial. The Biennial's a group show. A who's who of the art world: veterans like David Hockney, cult faves like Raymond Pettibon.

Altmejd had a room to himself. A monster morgue. I idled an hour away in it. A werewolf skeleton splayed on a slab.

Scratched in ink on its tibia: the word "CLIMB." On its fibula: "FALL." Had Altmejd autopsied his beasts? Did he find out what did them in?

Vanity. That's what I say. Who makes jewelry for werewolves? Hairy Winston? Should werewolves even wear jewelry? It's suicidal. A silver bullet can kill a werewolf—why can't a silver brooch?

2004

MIRRORS THAT MATTER

"The bird-men wear suits," David Altmejd says.

The bird-men are sculptures; Altmejd made them. They have human bodies; they have feathered heads and big beaks. I pull open a bird-man's blazer, looking for a label. The lining is rayon. No label.

"Every suit was bought at the Salvation Army," he tells me as he guides me through a gallery at the Art Gallery of Ontario. There are three bird-men in total: one towers atop a tall steel stage, one sits atop a mirrored room, the other stands beside me. I dust brush from the bird-man's blazer. His trousers are leather. "The leather pants come from a fetish store," he says.

Dust — it falls on the bird-men's feathers, it coats their coats. The gallery is full of it. It's a construction zone. The AGO is being rebuilt by Frank Gehry. Altmejd is installing "The Index," a sprawling sculptural installation that fills a room in the contemporary wing. The bird-men are part of The Index. They pose like dummies in a department store. Do they belong in the Menswear department, or in Pet Supplies?

Mirrors surround the bird-men. Small, large, cracked—there are mirrored platforms, mirrored display cases, mirrored walls that lead down mirrored halls. I step into the mirrored room. If I were Catholic, it might remind me of a confessional. I am no Catholic; I am a style writer. The room reminds me of a change room. Critics can read Altmejd's sculpture in countless ways: as a Borgesian labyrinth, as a museum of imaginary animals, as an exhibition of extreme sexuality. Me? Retail is my métier. The bird-men remind me of fashion mannequins. The mirrored display cases and changeroom remind me of fixtures at some strange store. A bizarre Barney's. A creepy Colette.

What is David Altmejd selling?

Altmejd is an art star. Born and bred in Montreal, he graduated with a master's degree from Columbia University in New York in 2001. When I met him in 2004, he had a sculpture in the Whitney Biennial, a dead werewolf sprouting crystals as it decayed. He took me to stores he haunted around Herald Square, discount dealers who specialized in fake feathers and flowers. He bought a brooch with the word "ART" written in rhinestones.

Later that year, Altmejd staged his first solo show at the Andrea Rosen Gallery in Chelsea. The centrepiece was a mirrored display case full of werewolf corpses. Gold chains wound like worms through fur. It was gorgeous and gruesome, as chic as a display at Chanel, but troubling, too. The sculpture concealed as much as it revealed: it contained crannies, staircases, crisscrossing corridors. Where a store would showcase a handbag, Altmejd stuck a werewolf skeleton, or skull, or penis.

In 2007, Altmejd represented Canada at the Venice Biennale. He constructed two sculptures, including "The Index," which will be on permanent display when the AGO reopens this week. He granted me a sneak peek. "The Index" reflects his continuing fascination with the speciousness of surfaces: his crystals are craft store glitter; his flowers are faille. For the first time I can recall, he incorporates clothing into his sculpture. Bird-men model menswear, secondhand styles from the Sally Ann. If clothes make the man, I wonder, what kind of clothes make bird-men? I ask Altmejd if he ever wore these suits. He says no. He doesn't seem interested in the clothes. It's the mirrors that matter.

Mirrors are womanly. A century ago, it was common for women to keep looking glasses on their vanities. In the 1920s and 30s, it was fashionable for women of wealth to wall their dressing rooms in mirrors. Department stores offered mirrored fitting rooms for their female clientele. Menswear departments didn't have change rooms; men took clothes home to try on, and took them to tailor shops to be altered.

Men ventured into mirrored rooms only at carnivals. *Glaces à répétitions* were mirrors that reflected themselves infinitely. A carnival-goer could enter a triangular mirrored room through a trapdoor; in the *glaces à répétitions*, he seemed to be hundreds of men. Carnival magicians used mirrored cabinets to make women and animals vanish. Carnival sideshows used angled mirrors to make disembodied heads speak. Fortune tellers summoned spirits in mirrors.

"The Index" combines the craftiness of the carnival with the seductiveness of the department store. It's a world of femininity and fakery in which mirrors, and not clothes, are tools of transformation. Men don't recognize themselves in their reflections; rather, they see men who are becoming animal, becoming mineral, becoming monstrous. Men metamorphose like females, like fashion. Altmejd's mirrors possess magic energies. The heart of "The Index" is the change room; in a way, the entire sculpture is a changeroom. Men don't change in it; men are changed by it.

2009

THE WOLF MAN'S MAGIC WORLD
An Interview with David Altmejd

"Why not fashion?" David Altmejd asks me.

Why not, indeed? I'm a fan of fashion; he's a fan of fashion.
When I went to interview him about the spectacular sculptures he
creates, we decided that fashion would offer a fine entrée to a
conversation.

Fashion feeds his work. Clothing, jewelry and wigs pop up in
in his sculptures. Bird-men sport natty suits. Rhinestone flowers
sprout from the corpses of werewolves. Gold chains swarm like
insects through mirrored counters and cabinets. The fashion world
furnishes him with many of his materials; he transforms them into
the flora and fauna of a world that's entirely his own design.
It's small surprise that fashion designers—Marc Jacobs and Raf
Simons, to name a few—admire his work. They're not alone: his art
is both original and engaging, critically-acclaimed and crowd-
pleasing. At thirty-seven, he is an artist of international stature, his
work collected by the Whitney Museum, the Guggenheim, the Dallas
Museum of Art and the National Gallery of Canada, among others.

Altmejd was born and bred in Montreal. He started his
studies at the Université du Québec à Montréal, then completed
them at Columbia. Though he has been in New York since
graduating, he still speaks with a Francophone accent. He apologizes
for his English. He shouldn't. He speaks well. Better still, his ideas
are as idiosyncratic and as his sculptures.

I met him almost a decade ago. If fashion is the framework for our interview, so too has it been a framework for our friendship. We talk about style. We go shopping together. He has much nicer clothes than I do. In my novel 'The Show That Smells', fashion icons Coco Chanel and Elsa Schiaparelli battle for the soul of a country singer. He created the novel's cover art, a crystal-encrusted werewolf head with tufts of shocking-coloured hair. For those who know fashion, the cover makes it clear: Schiaparelli wins.

ART IS A BROOCH THAT YOU WEAR ON A BLOUSE

DM: Years ago, when we first met, we walked around midtown Manhattan looking for costume jewelry for you to use in your work. You bought a brooch with the word ART in rhinestones. What happened to that?

DA: I don't think I used it. It would be too obvious.

DM: Still, it would look perfect on a blouse, don't you think?

DA: It depends on what blouse, and who is wearing it. It would be cool on an older lady.

DM: I'm an older lady. Can I have it?

(Laughter)

DM: I mention the ART brooch because brooches, and jewelry in general, play a big role in your work.

DA: I really use a lot of jewelry.

DM: I'm a fan of fashion and I'm fascinated by the way your work incorporates clothing and jewelry; I'm fascinated, too, by the way it plays with display and merchandising principles—plays with them and perverts them.

DA: I'm interested in display. It's not the main aspect of my work. It's an aspect among other aspects. I'm not even against the idea of using the same sort of strategies as stores. I've never really taken things from store display; I mean, I've never walked into a store and thought, I'll do that, I'll do that. I end up using the same strategies that stores do. I feel as if I do it instinctively.

DM: Where do you find your jewelry?

DA: I used to go to these wholesale stores where they hand you a basket when you walk in. You could buy a brooch for two dollars. I don't buy jewelry pieces anymore; instead, I buy the parts of them, the chains, the stones. It's more like I take the parts and put them together my own way.

DM: Do you ever incorporate precious jewels in the work?

DA: No, it's costume jewelry. I do use real crystals now, though, real rocks. I will use real amethysts. But precious stones, no—I don't need a diamond, I can use a fake diamond. It's not how much it's worth that matters, it's the effect.

DM: How about when galleries or museums stage shows of jewelry? Does that interest you at all, the work of jewelers?

DA: Yes, I am interested in beautiful artifacts, of course. I'm not so interested in the history part of jewelry, the chronology of creators and what was made. I like individual pieces. When I am really working on something, I feel as if I'm a jeweler making jewelry.

DM: When you're constructing a sculpture, what dictates where a piece of jewelry will go? Is it a sense of rightness?

DA: It's symmetry. I like things to be symmetrical, or at least balanced. Since we're talking about fashion, I will says this: it's sort of like a designer staring at a model and putting that final touch to her outfit, that final accessory, and saying, "That's it!"

(Laughter)

DM: Can jewelry be art?

DA: Yes, I think so. It's more likely to be art than fashion is. I can see a jeweler completely absorbed in his work and forgetting about what the purpose of it will be. It seems like a fashion designer would always be thinking of what the final result will be, which is people wearing his clothes.

DM: Can fashion be art?

DA: It's a different game. Fashion is much more respectful of taste. Even if it pushes boundaries, it's always tasteful; even when it tries to be distasteful, it's tasteful. In art, it feels like you can push it further.

DM: A designer can do something outrageous, but he still needs customers who want to wear the outrageous clothes, and who can pay for them.

DA: I think the idea of cool is important in fashion; I feel that when fashion designers do something outrageous, it's supposed to become cool right away. With art, there's the hope that it will remain outrageous or shocking, at least for a while.

49

DM: Fashion works at a frantic pace. The most shocking look is meant to be recuperated at a ferocious speed. Art, too, can be recuperated right away, too, but sometimes it isn't; sometimes it stays difficult and unsettling for a while.

DA: I feel like art is different, it's so conceptual in a way that it lets you do anything; whereas fashion is not really conceptual. When it says that it is, as with Hussein Chalayan, it's not true; it's really a style, it's the conceptual in quotation marks. It's the look of conceptual. I'm sorry, sometimes there are moments when my English is really, really bad.

WEREWOLVES DON'T WEAR SILVER PINS

DM: I met you in 2004, when you were in the Whitney Biennial.

DA: You wrote an article about me and called it "Hairy Winston."

DM: That was about the time you bought the ART brooch. I thought it might wind up in a werewolf sculpture. I thought: Don't put a silver brooch in a werewolf!

DA: I didn't.

DM: At that time, you were making sculptures with decaying werewolves. The werewolves were covered with costume jewelry and crystals.

DA: Jewelry, because it's shiny, it vibrates visually; I see it as something that has a little pulse. If you place it on something that's obviously dead, it's going to seem like a strange organ that generates real energy.

DM: The werewolf sculptures weren't really about dying and decay at all; they were about alchemy. Jewelry and crystals were somehow produced by the processes of death; they were growing. They were magic.

DA: Maybe it was magical. I like to think of it as physical, as biological. The jewelry plays a part in the transformation. Gold chain, for example, I use to connect elements. I see it as a way of making energy travel from one point to the other.

DM: It's the energy, but also the conduit. The jewelry refracts and redirects energy, but it also consists of energy. It's playing different roles in different situations. I love that, I love that its functions can change so fast. I also love that the jewelry doesn't have to be a diamond; it can be some dumb dime-store rhinestone.

THE SLOT IN A BOX THAT A RING SITS IN

DM: In 2004, at your first solo show at Andrea Rosen Gallery, there were lots of werewolves and jewelry. The show seemed to me to be at least a little bit about jewelry display.

DA: I remember a sentence you told me, something that you were going to put in your book. You said the slit in the head of a penis was like the slot in a jewelry box that a ring sits in.

DM: That line's your fault. In that first show of yours, dead werewolves doing all sorts of sexual things; no, it had werewolves who had died doing all sorts of sexual things. Or were they dead? I don't know. They were covered in gold chains and costume jewelry and they were lying in incredible mirrored boxes and counters.

DA: How do you activate an object? If you're given a werewolf head, how are you going to make it feel precious? For a really long time in my work, that was an important part of my work: to position them in such a way that they would vibrate. I don't think there's an infinite number of ways.

DM: I know that the chains and jewelry were acting as energy, and it made sense to me to think about retail: there are few places more fraught with energy and desire than store counters. I don't know what kind of store sells dead werewolves, or uses them as jewelry trays.

DA: I don't know.

DM: You were saying?

DA: If we think of the idea of activating an object, how do we do it? If you place it on a table, right in the center to make it look important, yes, people are going to think about store display. Throughout history, how did churches display sacred objects? A little bit the same way. It's not necessarily about store display; it's about making something seem precious.

THE CHANGEROOM CHANGES

DM: At the 2007 Venice Biennale, you used mannequins in your sculptures.

DA: Yes, but I haven't done it very often, only in that piece. And they had bird heads.

DM: I think it was the first time you incorporated clothing into your sculpture, wasn't it?

DA: A couple of the werewolves I made years ago had underwear and shoes. I made the underwear dirty to make sure that it was sort of decaying with the body. Becoming part of the body. It was involved in whatever transformation was happening with the body. I wanted them to wear a specific brand of underwear, which was 2Xist. It's a popular brand: if you go to a department store, you have a choice between Calvin Klein, 2Xist and Hugo Boss. I wanted to allude to existential ideas, but through underwear.

(Laughter)

DM: The mannequins in Venice couldn't help but conjure a retail space, David, at least in my mind. Not the Men's department, but the Bird-Men's. Do you like mannequins?

DA: I don't think I've ever loved a dress or piece of clothing that was worn by a mannequin. I never stop at a store window to look at what mannequins are wearing. It's dead. It's not cool if it's not worn by something dead; that's just my opinion.

DM: So with the mannequins, did you mean to convey a degree of deadness?

DA: If I had them wear clothes, it was sort of to make them seem more alive. It sounds contradictory. Putting a mannequin under clothes won't make the clothes look more alive; putting clothes on a mannequin makes the mannequin look more alive.

DM: Did you dress the mannequins in any particular designer's clothes?

DA: I don't remember. I used some new clothes and also some used ones. I didn't want them to look too much like they were in a store window.

DM: There was one bird-headed man in a booth that contained crystals and mirrors. It seemed to me to be a change room. Maybe he was trying on clothes, maybe he was changing from man to bird, or from bird to man. I considered that it could be a confessional booth, but it's mirrored, and that's really a retail thing.

DA: The mirrors are cracked and shattered. There are a lot of mirrors in stores and in display, but you don't look at yourself in them; it's not like the mirror is a focus that puts you at the centre. Of course the mirrors on the walls are there for you to look at when you try your pants on. The mirrors that line counters and are on columns are not looked at. Mirrors are materials that move and that multiply space and that vibrate visually. Do churches use mirrors? If I were to build a cathedral, I would place mirrors everywhere in it.

BEES ARE NATURE'S BROOCHES

DM: "The Vessel" and "The Swarm," a pair of huge sculptures, dominated your 2011 show at Andrea Rosen. They were giant Plexiglas boxes filled with insects, plaster hands and ears and yards of thread—thread fanning out, rising and falling, doubling back through holes, wrapping around shelves and objects. Was this the first time you used thread?

DA: There are a few pieces that I made previous to the show that used thread; but, no, I had never used it a lot before. It came about it as an alternative to gold chain. You know, the pieces you mentioned earlier, the big Plexiglas boxes with webs and networks of gold chain. I started using thread as a way to introduce colour.

DM: You dyed them?

DA: Yes, some of them have a gradation of thread. I painted them. I painted a bunch of threads with very diluted acrylic to create gradations that I wanted.

DM: The bees and the jellyfish you made from thread and Plexiglas—those struck me as the closest thing to jewelry I've seen you make.

DA: I really liked the insects. They are positive insects, insects that give. Not like ticks; ticks only take. I'm into using things that give and give and give: things that are generators. Bees give and pollinate flowers. Oh, it sounds so cheesy. (Laughter) I want everything in my work to generate. I want everything in my work to be generated inside the work. If there's gold chain, I want it to be coming from something, so I need a generator of gold chain at the beginning of the gold chain segment; it has to be coming from something that generates gold chain. It has to be coming from somewhere. That's why I used those little Plexi bees, the chain generator. If there's thread, it also has to be generated by something, that's why I like spools. There were a lot of spools in that show as well, because they're thread generators.

DM: What generates the spools?

DA: The spools are all handmade in Plexiglas. They're the same material as the box. In my mind, they're a mutation of the Plexi box that contains them.

DM: When I saw those Plexi boxes, I thought, it's offering a cross-section of what's happening in those rooms; there's no dead space where nothing is happening. There's also something happening. You made a box that lets us see what's happening all the time.

DA: The purpose of the box is as a support structure to give me the chance, because it's transparent, invisible, it gives me the chance to attach things and make them seem like they're floating.

DM: The spools are the same Plexiglas as the box: it's as though you had something rare, and put it in a display case or window, and the case and window started generating what was inside it.

DA: I like those shifts. I like to use something as a frame, and pretend it doesn't exist, then all of a sudden it starts to exist. In one of the pieces, I pretended that the box was just an invisible support, and all the Plexiglas structure that I added inside did not exist. In terms of one specific narrative, the Plexi isn't there, it's simply a support. At the end I added some ants and the ants started walking on the Plexi. For me that was the moment when the structure starts existing. They're not ignoring it. They're using it to get around. Again, from the beginning, the box doesn't exist, but it does sometimes. I like to go from pretending it's not there to using it and then going back to pretending again.

DM: It showed in the work, because it was like you were viewing an exhibit, but then you'd notice that the Plexi was fractured and it was participating in the piece.

DA: I liked the fractures in it. It's participating in the process of creation. I see it as something playful.

THAT NECKLACE IS WEARING YOU

DM: If jewelry can function that way in your sculptures, does the shininess function the same way on people?

DA: I think that the jewelry offers transformative powers. I'm really interested in the positioning of jewelry on people. It's not random. It's not random, for example, with a necklace. It hits right here, in the centre of the chest.

DM: Jewelry is close to perfume: it's worn it where you would wear perfume, behind the ears, on the wrists, at the base of the throat. Where there's heat and blood.

DA: Yes, but you don't need heat to make jewelry glitter, you only need light. I think it has more to do with the fact they're on sensitive areas. It's the same with the bindi; it's in an amazing position. Earrings—I question the importance of that. Do you think that's a good placement? Lip piercings, I think, are an abomination. They show a total disrespect, or lack of care. They're lazy. There's nothing that happens there. There's something too soft about the lips. Often when there's a piercing there, it's not in the centre, it's off to the side. I think tongue piercings are interesting—I mean, I don't like them, because they make me feel pain.

DM: Perhaps that's what some people want to do with their piercings: to make other people says, 'Ouch, ouch, ouch.'

DA: I don't have any piercings, I don't think I could have any. I would imagine that getting a piercing—I can imagine wanting a piercing if I wanted to take control of my body. 'David, your body is just skin and flesh, you can pierce it, you'll see, you'll feel you have control over it, it's not a bad deal. Don't worry, David, you can do what you want.'

DM: You've never felt the need to get control of your body that way?

DA: Maybe it would be an amazing feeling.

DM: You don't wear jewelry.

DA: No, but I like the idea of wearing it. I don't wear it probably because I feel like it's underlining my body. It's making it obvious that I have a body. If I wear a necklace or bracelet, it's going to be like saying, 'Hey, look at me, I'm here.' It would make me uncomfortable.

DM: It makes you uncomfortable that people would see that you are not invisible. Invisibility is important to you.

DA: It's not that it's important to me; it's simply a fact. I have always felt invisible, ever since I was a child. I mean, I know I am visible to you, but to most people I am not. I can walk down a street and not be noticed.

DM: That's a terrible feeling for a child to feel.

DA: It was hard. I always had the feeling that I would grow up and have—I don't want to say revenge, because that's not it. I had the sense that I would show everybody, you know? I thought that because I was invisible I could go anywhere and nobody would care. It was an opportunity to think and to become critical.

DM: And you still feel this way.

DA: Absolutely.

DM: So jewelry would compromise your invisibility? It would be akin to the Invisible Man putting on a bowtie?

DA: I would be invisible, but people would notice the jewelry. Jewelry has no purpose other than to be noticed. It's always an exclamation. It's always showy.

DM: What about clothes, then? How do you decide what to wear?

DA: Clothes are different than jewelry. Clothes can either draw attention or they can make you invisible. I always wear things that accentuate my invisibility.

DM: How can clothes accentuate invisibility?

DA: Well, it's a matter of avoiding things that are trendy. In terms of colour and cut... (pause) Oh, I have an honest answer but I've never talked about these things. I have codes, I have systems, but I don't know if I can put them into words.

DM: I think a lot of gay guys develop ideas like yours as boys, that they're invisible or monstrous or evil in some way. Me, I would rather be invisible than be disgustingly ugly, which is what I've always been.

DA: You have never been disgustingly ugly!

DM: You have never been invisible! It's difficult for me to comprehend all this, David, seeing as you're so good-looking. You have sex, David; you have boyfriends. Men notice you. Men see you.

DA: I don't believe they do. It's always dark when I would meet them.

(Laughter)

DM: I can't help but think of your 2008 show at Andrea Rosen, which featured colossi. These were giant statues, David, giant figures.

DA: Yes.

DM: You're invisible, yet you build statues of yourself that dominate the gallery. And some of them were made of mirrors, though they didn't function as mirrors: they somehow demanded and deflected attention.

DA: That's why I'm a sculptor. I think that it's very satisfying to make sculptures so that I can create things that aren't invisible. My physical and visual anchors in the world are my sculptures. The mirrors in the figures were sort of deflecting attention, which was a different level.

DM: It must be very unnerving when people criticize your work.

DA: But at the same time, there's something really satisfying about it—it's a reminder that I exist. I mean, no one would ever criticize me or my body because I'm invisible. It would never happen. It's amazing to know that I really exist in the world through those sculptures.

DM: They represent you, but you also understand that they're stand-ins for you.

DA: I can't back away from them. I don't want to. I don't like seeing that. I like being aware that people are looking at my work, but I don't want to see it happening. It gives me a sort of vertigo. It's not supposed to be like that. It would be like being outside of my body and seeing people looking at it. It's embarrassing.

DM: So your sculptures are you; that is, they are visible, tangible things that allow you to have a visible presence. You have taken all sorts of shapes: decaying werewolves covered in crystal; mirrored mazes people bird-headed men; Plexiglas boxes that contain ecosystems of thread and insects. All these Davids wear jewelry, though you do not; all these Davids are showy, though you are not. The boxes are invisible structures, though they can become visible; I could describe you the same way, too.

DA: Yes.

DM: The sculptures are always bursting with life. The energy—your energy—doesn't die; it's always pulsing and mutating.

DA: I'm wondering if with time it will change. I can imagine a piece so dusty that the energy will be held inside. What happens if the jewelry gets tarnished? What if it doesn't shine? Does it mean that the piece is dead? Does it have the same power? Is the magical aspect only connected to the shininess?

DM: Who in the world would let their David Altmejd get dusty?

DA: I'm not worried. I don't think that dust can kill anything.

2011

ATOMISED

Is fragrance a language? Are the components of perfume—the notes, fixative and solvent—the same as words in a sentence? Perhaps perfumes are poems or novels. What sort of novel smells? A book is paper; it smells like a perfume strip that has yet to be perfumed.

Fragrance may not be a language, but language is part of fragrance. When fashion houses release perfumes, they also release reams of words in the form of press copy and ads. The language is mostly stale: perfume is romance, love, mystery.

Balenciaga, the fabled French design house recently released Balenciaga L'Essence, and Nicolas Ghesquière, the house's creative director, came to New York City to talk about it. He mentioned neither romance nor mystery nor love.

"It's important to do something new," he says.

Since starting at Balenciaga in 1997, Ghesquière has made himself a figurehead for those who feel fashion should pioneer the future. He creates clothes and accessories that combine forward-thinking silhouettes with forward-thinking fabrics.

His forays into fragrance are relatively recent. Balenciaga L'Essence is the second scent he's co-created; the first, Balenciaga Paris, was released last year. He worked on both of them with perfumer Olivier Polge.

"I was completely new to that world," he says "I had no idea what the process was." So he went to school. Coty, the perfume company that produces Balenciaga's scents, taught him how perfumes are concocted, and to which families they belong: the *chypres*, the *floraux*, the *fougères*. "I learned so much about the vocabulary. One of the things I love is *sillage*, which is what is left from someone walking by, what stays in the room when someone's left. It's what makes men whistle at you." He laughs.

Ghesquière's affection for words comes through in his concept for L'Essence, which sounds like a piece of speculative fiction, or speculative fashion. The fragrance, he says, "is like a cut, you can linger over it indefinitely."

A cut?

"Fragrance should be something organic," he continues, fleshing out the analogy. "Something deeply organic that comes from the body, and that's used to make something else."

He pictures the perfume as a material that originates in the body, as blood originates in a wound or a mineral does in a mine. It is then transformed into fragrance and put back on the body. What, then, is a scab? A sort of sequin? A brooch of dried blood?

"It's quite fascinating when you think what will be. Will medicine and fragrance become the same? Will clothing and the body become the same? In every good Philip K. Dick book there is that thing, that body that becomes one with technology, that's a true hybrid. We are very far from that in fashion, unfortunately. Technology is one thing; there is not yet a real revolution in texture and fabric that's making a true difference. It's still design, a design performance."

For him, fashion designers fall into one of two camps. There are those who do collage—they apply colour and fancywork to standard shapes—and there are those who surround the body in new shapes. Cristóbal Balenciaga, the house's founder, was a builder, an obsessive architect of clothes. Ghesquière uses application in the service of construction. When he incorporates formica, as he did in his collection for F/W 2010, it's not simply as ornament. He sews it to silk; together, the formica and silk are an entirely new entity, a concretion that will, he predicts, come to seem natural in time.

Futuristic—this is how critics describe his clothes. It's a word he could do without. "When I read "futuristic" about my work, I get a little bit nervous. It's so easy to say that."

"Ghesquière's clothes are bold, graphic and very much of their time," says Mairi Mackenzie, author of *Isms: Understanding Fashion*, "but because some of his designs have utilized elements that are familiar to us from representations of the future in science fiction, he is therefore categorized in this way. I also think—to paraphrase a well-known saying—that to some extent, every generation recreates the future in its own image."

According to Ghesquière, the clothes he creates are contemporary, as are the ideas they embody. While he recognizes that they can seem robotic or fantastic, he believes that, like science-fiction literature, they're proposing something radically new for the present. His clothes don't presage the future so much as they simply presage the fact that there will be a future, and that it will be drastically different. He mentions that a favourite writer of his is Michel Houellebecq, the French dystopian novelist and essayist whose book *The Elementary Particles* was originally translated into English as *Atomised*. Which sounds like it might be a book about scent. It's not.

"I wore fragrance when I was a teenager, of course," he says. "My first one was a Karl Lagerfeld fragrance. It had a silver ring on the stopper. It was called Karl Lagerfeld Pour Homme. Karl once told me, 'That was my wedding ring for men.'"

Ghesquière grew up in Loudun, a small town in western France. As a teenager, he apprenticed at agnes b. and Jean Paul Gaultier. He became the designer at Balenciaga at the old age of twenty-six.

"It used to be a beautiful fashion house," he says of Balenciaga, "but also a fragrance house with a tradition of scents, so it would be great if we could give a little of that today. To do something new that has a reminder of this patrimony."

What has he done? Balenciaga Paris was a chypre floral.

Violet leaves provided the dominant scent, while violets themselves took a backseat. Balenciaga L'Essence is greener still. While violet leaves predominate, metallic notes are sharper. Despite that, it has a woodsy tone.

It is lovely, for sure; but is it something new?

The radicalness of it isn't in the smell, but in the story that Ghesquière has given it, that the perfume is a hybrid of the body's essence and scent. It's "science-fictionish," to use his term, which is apt: perfume and words work together in science-fictionish ways.

"There are certain experiences that cannot be described," says Richard Stamelman, author of *Perfume: Joy, Obsession, Scandal, Sin*, a book-length investigation into fragrance and language. "Perfume must be experienced in person, and many people don't live in places where they can do that. They read about it in magazines first, or see ads. Words carry it to them."

Ghesquière conceptualized what sort of scent he wanted made. He described it to a perfumer, who translated it into scent. A press agent described it to a journalist, who transmits it to a readership. At the end of this, a reader sniffs the perfume in a magazine, or she stops at a store to smell the scent. Until she can smell it, the fragrance is something linguistic; it consists of adjectives and analogies; it is ink or black bytes on a screen. Fragrance is immaterial, so its particles adhere to words as they do to skin and fabric. Words become olfactory particles.

As Ghesquière says, "It is a very difficult process to name a new thing. That's why writers are so important."

Writing is perfume's foremost visual form, though far from its only one. There is advertising, too: Charlotte Gainsbourg is the face of Balenciaga L'Essence's advertising campaign. There is the bottle: L'Essence comes in the same glass bottle that Paris came in. Ghesquière calls it a "matrix:" the bottle stays the same, while the colour and scent of its content changes.

I received the fragrance in a silver tester bottle. The tester came in a shiny black sack, which I have with me at the interview.

All fragrance samples, Ghesquière says, come in sacks sewn from similarly shiny fabrics. It's standard in the industry. The sparkliness of the sack, it seems, is supposed to capture the effervescence of the scent.

"That is organdy," he says, trying to identify which fabric the sack's sewn from. "To tell you the truth, it's not really organdy." He studies it, its moiré pattern. "Organdy is cotton and organza is silk. This is polyester. This is organzyester!"

He laughs. The designer of hybrids has designed a hybrid word.

2011

THE FLORALS OF EVIL

I have never gone to an orgy; I've never been invited. No matter—I don't have to be a libertine to smell like a libertine.

Les Liaisons Dangereuses by Kilian is an orgy in a perfume bottle, a fragrance steeped in the scents of group sex. Or so claims Kilian Hennessy, the perfumer who produced it for By Kilian, his upscale, upstart Parisian perfume house.

"Bodies slick with sweat, hot with the odors of sexual favours," is how Hennessy describes his perfume in promotional material. Sounds swell to me; I'm lonely. But is it prostitution or perfume? Sweat, saliva, secretions of all description—does anybody besides me want to smell of sexual favours? Does anybody want to pay by the ounce for sex?

Mais oui! In the world of perfume, sex is selling. Perfume counters at posh stores are crowded with the scents of coitus. There is French Lover by Editions du Parfum; Putain des Palaces, or Hooker of the Hotels, by État Libre d'Orange; Querelle by Parfumerie Générale, named for the Jean Genet novel about a homicidal sailor in a seaside brothel. It was widely reported that Tom Ford wanted Black Orchid, his first fragrance, to smell "like a man's crotch."

Sex, drugs, and druggy sex—these are the themes of L'Oeuvre Noir, or the Black Masterpiece, Kilian Hennessy's first collection of scents. The collection is an homage to the *poètes maudites*, the nineteenth-century's foremost literary libertines—Baudelaire, Verlaine, Rimbaud.

"Did Baudelaire wear a scent?" I say.

"I don't know," Hennessy says to me. He's in Toronto to promote his perfumes. "I believe he spent money on opium, not perfume."

"Still, isn't it strange to sell a perfume based on the smell of Rimbaud?" I say. "Rimbaud never washed. I'm sure he smelled like hell."

"But this is not the smell of Rimbaud," he says. At thirty-five, he is suave and slender, suited in Dior by Hedi Slimane. Black eyes, black hair, black blazer. "This is about the passions that possessed them.

"L'Oeuvre Noir contains six perfumes," he says, arranging bottles on a table. The bottles are black, as are the boxes they come in. "There are two perfumes inspired by ingénues, by beautiful young women or men. Scents of temptation. There are two inspired by *les paradis artificiels*, by opium dens and absinthe. And there are two inspired by Parisian orgies."

"Soft and hard," he says. "In each pair of perfumes, there is a soft perfume, and a hard." He dips a scent strip in Les Liaisons Dangereuses by Kilian, the softer of the orgy scents. I smell it. Sandalwood and cinnamon make it spicy; musks make it amatory. Cruel Intentions by Kilian is the hard orgy perfume. He wets a scent strip with it. "Oudh," he says, passing it to me. Oudh is resin secreted by a rare South Asian tree. "Very woodsy, very warm," he says, smiling slyly. "You feel safe, and then—an animalic note springs out. And you're trapped."

"It is a classic French way to make perfume," he says, referring to animalic scents, the basest base notes. Civet oil, which is drawn from the anal gland of the civet cat, and which is said to smell a bit like blood. Castoreum, the animalic note in Cruel Intentions by Kilian, which comes from a gland in the guts of a beaver. According to perfume critic Chandler Burr, it smells of "leather, urine, smokey tar, and of anus." "American perfumes are so often what we call 'overdoses,'" Hennessy says. "They have a single strong sent, sometimes soapy. Americans like clean scents. They smell like laundry sometimes. I am creating something darker."

The French are fond of animal aromas. Christian Dior's perfumers called Dioressence (1969) *le parfum barbare*—the barbaric perfume. It hit the nose hard with animalic and fecal notes. Miss Dior (1947) smelled a bit like sweaty armpits.

In Dior's day, perfumers and the ladies who purchased perfumes didn't discuss fecal and anal odours in public. Perfumery was an art shrouded in secrecy. Today, a company could put out these same Dior scents and call them Feces and Armpits. *Pourquoi pas?* Alan Cumming put out a critically-praised perfume called Cumming. It smells like it sounded.

Cumming is only the beginning. Putain des Palaces smells sort of slutty—lipstick and face powder in an old leather purse. Sécrétions Magnifiques, also by L'État Libre d'Orange, comes in a box emblazoned with a cartoon penis that's squirting semen. Dzing! by L'Artisan Parfumeur (the scent has been discontinued, but is still for sale) is rich with circus smells—sawdust, gasoline from generators, and wild animal dung.

The great French perfumer Jacques Guerlain once said that perfumes should smell "of the underside of his mistress." The scents he created, such as Jicky (1889) and Shalimar (1925), were tinged with vaginal and anal smells. Perfumers today build perfumes around accords of saliva and sweat, and advertise ejaculation. What is advertisement without semen? Images of sex and death inundate us in the media; perhaps the odors of sex and death are becoming less taboo. Perhaps culture has convinced people to become so clean, so antiseptic, that the smells of dirt and decay are desirable. Perhaps it is a *CSI* effect—people are fascinated with the forensics of blood, semen, decomposition. Or—perhaps it's all marketing.

"There are hundreds of perfumes released every year," Hennessy says to me. "For every five hundred, there are five successful ones." Before founding his own line of fragrances, he worked as a marketer for other perfume houses, including Christian Dior and Alexander McQueen. "People want to smell different than other people, they want their own perfumes." By giving his products naughty names and breathless backstories, he's making sure his perfumes get press. Perfume's biggest companies—Coty and Chanel, for example—don't name their brands for sluts and secretions. It's the niche perfumers like Hennessy.

"I know every scent there is," he says. "I know how to create them. Animalic notes have always been around, have always been at the disposal of the perfumer. The scents of decay, of death, they do not repulse me. There are scents I'd prefer not to smell—bad body odour on an airplane. But I'm not sickened by it." He smiles. "The only thing that sickens me are tacky perfumes. I am repulsed only by what is poorly made."

2008

DZING!

Dzing! It's a French perfume. I wet my wrist.

Dzing! by L'Artisan Parfumeur. It smells like shit. It's an animalic, a type of perfume with a fecal fragrance. When I sniff myself, I get a whiff of wet fur and asshole.

Dzing! smells like circus animals—lions, elephants, bears—and the shit they shit. I smell other smells in it, too. Sawdust. Leather saddles. Something sweet—cotton candy, caramel apples, or nuts.

The scents of a circus in a bottle. But can they be captured in a book?

The show that smells—this is what carnies and circus folk call an animal show. It's also what I named my new novel.

The Show That Smells is set at a circus.

There's a midway: the story's set entirely in a mirror maze.

There's fashion: Elsa Schiaparelli, the fabled fashion designer, is a vampire; Coco Chanel, the fabled fashion designer, is a vampire hunter.

There's perfume: Schiaparelli is selling Shocking!, a perfume whose base note is blood. When humans wear it, vampires can home in on them. Chanel is selling Chanel N° 5, a perfume impregnated with holy water. When humans wear it, they're impervious to vampire assaults.

I'm in it. I play a writer for *Vampire Vogue* magazine.

Vampires, carnivals, couture—*The Show That Smells* is full of these things, as was my previous novel, *The Haunted Hillbilly*.

In *The Haunted Hillbilly*, a vampire named Nudie made Hank Williams a star. He did so by making Hank Williams's suits: garish gabardines gussied up with sequins. The suits proved irresistible to the public: they glittered like the chalkware dolls that carnies used to give away at carnival games. Nudie made the sequins by boiling human bones.

In *The Show That Smells*, Elsa Schiaparelli sells Shocking! It's made with blood from babies. Her haunt is a mirror maze, the perfect place for a vampire to prey on people. Like a scent, she has no reflection—no one can see her coming! I like to think that the maze's mirrors are akin to facets in a crystal flaçon. Is being in a mirror maze something like being in a perfume bottle?

The Haunted Hillbilly starred Hank Williams, country music's most famous singer. *The Show That Smells* stars Jimmie Rodgers.

In 1927, a nobody named Jimmie Rodgers walked in a hat warehouse in Bristol, Tennessee. He had on a business suit and a boater.

He'd come to sing, not to shop. The Victor Recording Co. had set up a recording studio in the warehouse, hoping to find local hillbillies to make hillbilly records. Jimmie wasn't local.

He hailed from Meridian, Mississippi. He was, however, a hillbilly.

He sang some sentimental songs that sounded folksy. Victor released them. They sold strongly. At a Victor studio in New Jersey, he sang several more. "T for Texas"—also known as "Blue Yodel"—was one of them. It became a monster, a million seller. Jimmie Rodgers became a star. He toured with Will Rogers. He recorded with Louis Armstrong. He shot a short movie in Hollywood: he strummed and sang before a backdrop of a railroad shack. Before being a singer, he'd been a railroad man, a brakeman on the Mobile & Ohio. "The Singing Brakeman," Americans came to call him. Also: "The Mississippi Blue Yodeler" and "America's Blue Yodeler." He yodeled the same yodel in almost every record he cut.

He wasn't the only act discovered in Bristol. Days after he recorded his first records, a singing family showed up at the studio: the Carter Family.

"He loved the hillbillies, the same as he loved the common people everywhere," said Carrie Rodgers in her memoir, *My Husband, Jimmie Rodgers*, "and loved to be among them and with them."

More than that, Jimmie loved circuses and carnivals. As a kid, he ran off with a circus. The big top: bedsheets he borrowed from his brother's wife. The big act: him, singing. He sang in Meridian, then tramped to another town. By the time his brother caught him, he'd made enough to buy new bedsheets. He ran away again. Local children were the circus acts. His tent was store-bought, charged to his father's account without his father's knowing it.

In 1925, he was a struggling singer, driving around Dixie in a street show. Having bought an interest in the operation, he brought a carnival on board. It included a Hawaiian show: girls in grass skirts dancing daringly. Did it include games or rides? Did it include a freak show? An animal show? Books about Jimmie don't say. What they do say: the carnival was destroyed in a blowdown, which is carny slang for a big windstorm.

"Big Circus Tent"—this was the name of a show he headlined in 1930. He toured it through the south. He shared the bill with "Miss Helene, Mentalist." The bigtop was red and contained a calliope, a "colored orchestra," and, of course, hundreds of seats. Beyond the bigtop was a complete carnival, including rides, a midway, barking barkers and minstrel shows. Jimmie's dressing room was a tent with screens and roll-up walls. And a bed. After a show, he had to rest. It took him an hour to remove his make-up. He was dying of tuberculosis. He had a pricy collection of perfumes from France. He would sniff them—it killed the stink of sick rising from his lungs.

Narcisse Noir by Caron.

It was Jimmie Rodgers's favourite perfume. In the United States, it was sold as Black Narcissus. The top note was orange blossom; the bottom, black narcissus.

Jimmie's nose was full of the fragrance of his liquefying lungs. I'm sure he would have loved a perfume that smelled like something sweet from his life. Like Carrie, or Carrie's vagina. Or a carnival.

Shocking! by Schiaparelli. It wasn't her first perfume, but it was her most famous. Introduced in 1937, it included notes of narcissus. Its animalic scents came courtesy of ambergris and civet. Ambergris is a waxy substance found in the stomachs of sperm whales. Civet is oil from the anus of a civet cat. Schiaparelli intended it to shock. Shocking! was supposed to smell like panties, like post-coital pussy. She titled her memoir *Shocking Life*. She named her favourite shade of pink "shocking pink." Shocking is also a sideshow word—"Shocking and Amazing! See the Living Vampire! See the Human Worm! See a Beautiful Girl Become a Gorilla!"

In 1938, Schiaparelli staged a circus in the street in front of her shop in Paris. Tightrope walkers trod high above the Place du Vendôme. Fire breathers breathed fire. Acrobats acrobatted.

In the shop, Schiaparelli showed her Circus Collection. It included a coat stitched with dancing horses, and closed with

83

acrobat-shaped buttons. Buttons on other ensembles were clowns. Handbags were shaped like balloons.

Sideshow freaks were Schiaparelli's main muses. She put monkey fur on boots and bracelets, an homage to the Girl-to-Gorilla sideshow act. The act is accomplished with mirrors. She printed crepe dresses with lobsters, which I interpret as a paean to Lobster Boys, men born with claws for fingers. She showed a Tear Dress, a dress with a trompe l'oeil pattern of tears and rips, as though it had been torn by a tiger in an animal show. The Skeleton Dress was a black dress that seemed to have bones—a spine and ribs stuck out from the fabric, making the wearer seem like a skeleton wrapped in a shroud. It was an homage to the Human Skeleton act. At a carnival or circus, the Human Skeleton was a man who was wasting away with tuberculosis.

What kind of *couturière* turns her clients into freaks?

Schiaparelli had a sinister sense of humour, for sure. In my novel, I make her a vampire. Is it so far-fetched?

Schiaparelli hated Chanel; Chanel hated Schiaparelli. Bad blood doesn't begin to describe it. Chanel refused to say Schiaparelli's name, let alone speak to her or of her. Which is why it shocked tout Paris when Chanel approached Schiaparelli at a costume ball in the 1930s. Chanel asked Schiap to dance. She waltzed Schiap across the floor. She dipped Schiap so that Schiap's hat came into contact with a candle. Schiap was on fire.

Burning a foe to death is barbaric. Unless your foe is undead.

In *The Show That Smells,* Schiaparelli is a vampiress who dresses the world's wealthiest women.

For her Carnival Collection, she shows apparel inspired by Human Skeletons and Lobster Boys. When the world's wealthiest women are dressed as sideshow acts, she will put them in a sideshow at a vampire carnival.

Her carnival will feature rides that vampires can revel in— haunted houses full of priests and nuns. It will feature games with prizes that vampires can prize—dolls made from dead babies stuffed with sawdust. Jimmie Rodgers will sing beneath the big top. She makes him a Faustian offer: he will be able to sing forever, so long as he becomes a vampire. What choice does he have? He is dying of TB. What makes his life bearable: the smell of Chanel N° 5, and Carrie.

Carrie Rodgers attempts to protect her husband from the vampires. It's a futile task, until the cavalry comes: Coco Chanel and the Carter Family. The Carters are formidable foes. Their signature song is "Keep on the Sunny Side." Chanel is the designer who made beachwear and suntanning fashionable. She made cross-shaped brooches and bangles fashionable. Coco was her nickname; her given name was

Gabrielle, as in the archangel. Only Christian Dior had a holier name. Then came Christian Lacroix.

In *The Show That Smells*, I describe Shocking! as smelling the same as Dzing!—sawdust, sugar, animal spoors. And blood. When women wear it, they smell like a vampire's supper. Vampires wear it, too.

Vampires love perfume, as they have no scents of their own. They don't have body odour; they don't perspire. They're dead, so they carry a trace of cadaverine. Dogs detect it. Vampires prefer perfumes that camouflage them: scents that smell like living rooms, or libraries, or late nights.

Vampires are peculiarly suited for perfume. Perfumes flower on people—they're transformed by the heat of bodies. Perfumes stay the same on vampires. Vampires have no blood, no body heat. They're smelling strips. Do this: smell *The Show That Smells*. It doesn't smell like paper. It smells like vampires perfumed as paper.

2008

MUGLER MANIA

I have made a breakthrough in the psychoanalytic study of
fags, or *psychofaganalysis*—thanks to Thierry Mugler.

At "Thierry Mugler: Couturissisme," a retrospective of his
oeuvre at the Montreal Museum of Fine Arts, I was able to
answer a question that has long plagued psychofaganalysts.

The question: Why do fags so often create fashion?

The answer: They don't create it; it creates them.

"Couturissime" displays more than 150 of Mugler's designs.
It includes runway showpieces, projections of runway shows
and music videos, and costumes he created for the Comédie-
Française, a theatrical company that's been around since Louis
XIV ruled France. It's accompanied by an adulatory catalogue
that lays out the facts of his career but doesn't even try to tell
us why fashion make fags.

Fashion makes fags so that fags make fashion.

"Since it is common knowledge that male homosexuals in
extraordinary numbers are involved in fashion-creation,"
Edmund Bergler wrote in *Fashion and the Unconscious* in 1953,
"there is a tentative discussion of whether or not the
unconscious hatred of women typical for every homosexual
has been responsible for some of the dress absurdities of the
last half-century."

Bergler was an analyst and an associate of Freud's who was
famous for his homophobia and for his fixation on fag fashion

designers. He believed that homosexuals dressed women as monsters.

Thierry Mugler is his nightmare.

"Couturissisme" is a monster mash. There are vamps, she-devils, glamazons. There's a chimera in golden armor and sequin scales. There's a fish woman in a fishtail gown with fins. There are women who appear to be wearing parts of Cadillacs—dashboards, fenders, lights—or who appear to be themselves Cadillacs.

Fagginess, Bergler believed, begins when a baby sees his mother as a monster who withholds comfort on a whim. The baby begins to find pleasure in being denied. To counter this masochism, he aggresses against her, then goes gay.

Presto!—a pervert.

"Couturissime" is a pervert's paradise. There are corsets. There are clothes that look tattooed or that are pierced with hoops and studs. Vinyl, rubber, queer *cuir*—there are materials to please almost every paraphilia. Mechanophilia: he designed robot bodices. Formicophilia: he designed a dress after an ant's carapace. Teratophilia: he designed a couture chimera in golden armor and sequin scales. Then there are dresses that mimic fish and shellfish. Are such creations acts of zoophilia, autozoophilia or overtures to vorarephilia?

What is Mugler's fetish?

Manfred Thierry Mugler was born in Strasbourg, France, and was raised there and in Vittel, near Nancy.

Nancy is a synonym for fag.

Mugler's father was a doctor. Mugler didn't become a doctor. His mother was a fashion plate who wore couture. He became a couturier.

Freud tells us that a fetish is the image of the final thing a subject sees before he sees his mother's missing phallus, shoes or underwear or pubic hair (which becomes fur or cloth in the fetishistic psyche). For Mugler, it was Chanel, Cardin or Courrèges: not cloth, not clothing, but high fashion, the hautest of the haute.

In my psychofaganalytic opinion, his fetish is fashion itself— constantly fleeting and fleetingly constant.

Mugler studied classical dance with the National Opera of the Rhine in Strasbourg, then moved to Paris. Fashion found him. He was a passive pervert, fetishizing clothes he saw on the streets, in the stores. In his mid-twenties, he turned from passive to active fag: he started creating clothes.

Though he had no formal fashion training, he started producing a prêt-a-porter line in his apartment-cum-studio in 1974. The earliest pieces in "Couturissime" date to 1978: unisex uniforms for some far-off planet's armed forces. They bear the influence of Stalin's tunics, sci-fi B-movies and Ronald Kolodzie, a designer who often outfitted Richie Gallo. Gallo was an American performance artist who looked like a sadomasochistic alien: the Martian who fell into the Mineshaft.

In 1979, David Bowie donned a glittering Mugler finned gown for his "Boys Keep Swinging" music video. It made Mugler the man of the New Wave moment. In 1980, the band Rough Trade released its first studio album. The album was art-directed by General Idea and it featured the front woman, Carole Pope, on the cover. She was butch as fuck in a militaristic Mugler coat. She sang about SM, drag, Nazism. On the single "Fashion Victim," she sang: "Montana, Fendi, Lagerfeld, Mugler, Kenzo, Chloé/We're all victims of fashion and accessories."

The album was called *Avoid Freud*.

Mugler got famous. By the early 80s, his shows were spectacles: he sold tickets to see them and thousands paid. Critics criticized him for being misogynistic—shades of Bergler's insistence that homosexuals hate women. Critics criticized him for his "Nazi" aesthetic—again, shades of Bergler and his insistence that *capos* at concentration camps were sadistic criminal homos.

Nazism was a weird accusation, considering that his signature suit—sharp shoulders, wasp waist, peplum—was an update of the Victory Suit that American women wore in World War II. It was weird, too, considering that his shows starred drag queens, club kids, and icons of pop music and porn: they were more Weimar than Wehrmacht. It was as if the degenerates had destroyed the Third Reich, becoming sleeker, stronger, more *super* in the process. *Arbeit macht* fierce.

In 1992, he presented haute couture for the first time. The couture in "Couturissime" is even pervier than the prêt-a-porter. There's a dress that's meant to hang from nipple piercings. There's a robe encrusted with Swarovski crystals on the inside: wouldn't it hurt to wear that? There's a riding-coat style suit whose décolletage is decorated with crystals that look like ice and faux-fur that looks like snow. Frozen fur—it's so Sacher-Masoch.

In 2002, Mugler left the fashion world to concentrate on directing cabarets and costuming Cirque du Soleil. He left behind an archive of thousands of singular garments. He also left behind a line of perfumes: Angel, his first scent, has been a bestseller since it was introduced more than two decades ago. Angel incorporates ethyl maltol, a compound that has long appeared in trace amounts in perfumes. In Angel, it's the top note. It smells like candy. The secondary notes aren't so sweet: deep patchouli and musk deliver a whiff of feces or Freud. Fetishes, Freud says, sometimes find a foothold in coprophilic smells.

What isn't Mugler's fetish? The man has a fetish for fetishes. Or is it a fetish for fetishes for fetishes? Or is it a fetish for fetishes for fetishes for fetishes?

Perversions, Bergler said, always work their way to the surface. Mugler multiplies perversions and then the perversions pervert perversions so that perversions spill perversely across the surfaces of his clothes like sperm.

Mugler affirms that fashion is the fabric of fagginess and that fagginess is the faggiest of all perversions. Bergler affirms the perfect circle of this perversion: Since fashion allows fags to dress women as monsters, then boys will always see their mothers as monsters. This means that there will always be gay boys. This means that there will always be gay boys who go into fashion. This means that *fashion—like fagginess—is forever*.

Italics are mine.

2019

THE MEN WHO FELL TO EARTH
An Interview with Joey Arias

What are more French than follies? The Folies Bergère, Moulin Rouge, the Lido—Paris is famous for its racy revues.

Then there's Mugler Follies. It's new: it had its debut earlier this week at the Théâtre Comédia near Montmartre. It's the creation of Manfred T. Mugler, better known as Thierry Mugler, designer, art director and bodybuilder (Manfred is his first name, and his preferred name nowadays).

Mugler Follies, Mugler's website says, is "a touching, shocking, beautiful, disconcerting event." Like all follies, it features nearly-naked showgirls (and showboys), acrobats, comedians. It also features cabaret icon and drag doyenne Joey Arias, Mugler's longtime muse and the original star of Zumanity, the Cirque du Soleil show for which Mugler made costumes.

Arias performed in Toronto recently as part of 'Bowie Is', the Art Gallery of Ontario's blockbuster exhibit about David Bowie. The exhibit included a video of Arias, along with his friend Klaus Nomi, singing backup for Bowie on 'Saturday Night Live' in 1979. It was Nomi's big break: he went on to become a cult icon for performing opera as if it were pop, and pop as if it were opera. It was Arias's big break, too. He was twenty. He was wearing Mugler.

DM: What is Mugler Follies?

JA: Mugler Follies is a production created and directed by Manfred T. Mugler. It has amazing performers, acrobats, singers and dancers, with imagery that is out of this world. Manfred has worked on this production for years. His script and songs are original. It's his show—he's worked on every detail.

DM: Is there a story to it, or is it strictly a revue?

JA: The storyline is: What we could do and where we could go if we followed our dreams? That's all I will say. My role will be Z Chromosome. I'm the new sex, neither he nor she. There's actually a hologram of me in the show—it took twenty-five hours a day of filming! I'll be there in Paris in the near future, as guest star.

DM: How did you meet Mugler?

JA: In 1980, Mugler was having a gigantic show in New York. He put out a casting call for models. Klaus Nomi and I met him and showed him all our photos and he said, "You have your own looks, but please be my guests at the show." As the years went by I'd see him, but I was very shy. And it wasn't until the end of the 1980s that we started seeing each other more, that he started coming to my gigs. And then he brought me on for "Too Funky," the George Michael video. After that we became the closest friends.

DM: So you were a Mugler fan before you worked with him?

JA: I was a Mugler freak since 1975 and followed everything he was doing. It was Mugler, Mugler, Mugler.

DM: You were wearing Mugler when you sang back-up for Bowie.

JA: Yes!

DM: How did the Bowie performance come to be?

JA: It was at the Mudd Club one night, it was like four o'clock in the morning, everyone was drunk and crazy. Klaus and I were leaving and we saw this smile coming from across the room—it was David. So we were trying to get past his bodyguards. I had this friend who was a Russian hitman. He was talking to a bodyguard, I don't know what he said, but suddenly we were whisked over to meet David. David went, "Oh, my God, Klaus Nomi? I love what you're doing, we need to talk!" And a day later David called Klaus. David wanted Klaus and Tony Basil to do something with him. I was working at Fiorucci at the time, and Klaus would tell me what was happening, and then finally, after two weeks, I think, Klaus said, "Everything's changed. He's doing *SNL*. He wants to know if you want to do the part." Yes, I said! So I painted Klaus's hair and I went and got my hair touched up.

DM: Where did you get your hair dyed red in those days?

JA: It was a place called Jingles in London. I was one of the first, if not the first, person in New York to have dyed hair. I dyed my hair in 1977. People were spitting at me, throwing rocks at me, trying to beat me up. I was chased all over Manhattan. Klaus was fifteen years older than I was. He was going bald already. It was Vidal Sassoon, a dear friend of ours, who cut out the triangles around his ears and started making it more angular.

DM: Bowie saw something in you and Klaus that he liked, obviously.

JA: David said to us, "This is like 1930s Berlin! This isn't an act, this is the real deal!" David said he wanted to sing "The Man Who Sold the World," "Boys Keep Swinging," and "TVC15." He wanted to do this whole German thing, riffing on Bauhaus and Nazism. The costume for "The Man Who Sold the World" was this Bauhaus suit that had been designed way back then.

"What are you guys going to wear?" he said to us. We said, "We can't wear what we do in our show." He gave us, like, $2000 each, and at that time, that was a million dollars. Every time Klaus and I went shopping, we couldn't afford anything. And when we finally had some money, we couldn't find anything.

DM: Where did you go?

JA: We went to Bergdorf Goodman, Charivari. We went to Macy's, Bloomingdale's. Those were the main stores where we could never buy clothes. Our last stop was Henri Bendel. We went up to the women's department. The saleslady had these Thierry Mugler dresses. She came out holding them in front of her, a black one and a red one. They were a hundred dollars each. We said, "It's for *SNL*, we can't tell you who we're singing with, but it's a rock star with one blue eye and one brown eye." We went back to the studio with these bags. David said, "Let's see," and we said, "No, we're going to put them on." So we went and changed. David said it was perfect, and it was. I had red hair, Klaus had black hair, and David's hair was white. "Red, white, and black, does that say something?" David said.

DM: It was a spectacular performance.

JA: Before the show Bowie said, "Tonight, we're going to make history. Your lives are going to change forever." He was right. It changed my life. It changed Klaus's life. Backstage after the show he introduced me to Nona Hendryx, Bette Midler, Iggy Pop. And Debbie Harry—she came to rehearsal, she said, "What I wouldn't give to be in your shoes!' I said, 'Debbie, you have Blondie; this is my time!"

DM: Do you still see Bowie?

JA: I saw David about ten years ago, before I joined Cirque du Soleil. We had dinner in Paris with Mugler and Iman and others; there were about ten of us. We talked for hours. We talked about *SNL*. We talked about what we're doing and where we're going. He said, "You look better than you did back then, did you have a sex change?" I said, "No, this is all me!"

2013

GOD'S GAULTIER
Dodie Bellamy Curates "Kathy Forest"

Kathy Acker's ghost. She's shopping in San Francisco. She stares into a window. A second-storey window. What she sees: garments floating, fluttering. Gaultier, Westwood, Comme des Garçons.

"This," she says to herself, "is the greatest store I have ever seen."

Kathy Acker's ghost moves among garments.

"Everything," she says, "is so me."

"Everything," she says, "fits like a dream."

As it should. The clothes are hers. Were hers. Kathy Acker died in 1997. Novelist, essayist, librettist—she left behind a beautiful body of work. She was also a shopper. She left behind a lot of labels.

"Too Young to Die, Too Fast to Live"—a slogan slapped on a Jean Paul Gaultier gown. Here: a Vivienne Westwood suit coat. There: a Norma Kamali body suits. Betsey Johnson babydolls. Yohji Yamamoto.

"This isn't a store," she says. She's right: it's an art gallery.

This isn't a store. It's a séance.

How to summon the spirit of a shopaholic? Display the clothing she loved.

Kathy Acker's ghost slips in and out of outfits. "Who did this?" she says. "Dodie?"

Dodie Bellamy, a brilliant poet and Acker's contemporary. She installed Acker's clothes at New Langton Arts Center in San Francisco this past summer. "Kathy Forest," she called the installation.

"We hung the clothes from fishing line," Bellamy tells me. "About twenty-five pieces, making sure there was enough space for people to walk between each piece. The clothes twirled in the breeze." Shirts, skirts, shrugs. "Our idea was a forest of clothes, and after the fact I named the exhibit." If this was a forest, where were the trunks? Trees don't twirl. Bodies do. Shades of a gallows. Shades of hangman's trees. Corpse copse.

Shades of many things. A weird window display. A Halloween haunted house. A spiritualist's salon where revenants roam. Bellamy was the medium. Q: What size dress did the spiritualist wear? A: Medium. Kathy Acker's ghost wafts among her wardrobe. She lived in these clothes. These clothes lived through her. She was, without a doubt, the most spectacularly-clad writer I've ever seen. Who she was wrapped up with what she wore.

I first came across Kathy Acker in an article in *The Face*, in 1984. Acker, said the magazine, "will wear wide, wide boiler suits over zipped and frilly nylon blouses, t-shirts exquisitely

slashed, sinister silver jewelry of cockroaches and skeletons."
Accompanying the article, a portrait of Acker by Robert
Mapplethorpe. She's in a sack of a sweater. Her favourite
designers, she said, were New York J.D.s (Juvenile
Delinquents), who "don't know much about the shape of the
body yet." "Street fashion is where the art is for poor people,"
she said. "I can't afford to buy a painting so if I get some
money, I go buy a dress."

In 1988, I saw Acker read from *Empire of the Senseless* in
Toronto. "[S]omewhat terrifying to behold" is how the *Toronto
Star* depicted her appearance. She was wearing Vivienne
Westwood, from the Fall & Winter 1988 collection. The "Time
Machine" collection, Westwood called it. A men's coat. Grey
pinstripes broken up by blocks of black. Sleeves were
detachable. Sleeves were stitched together from what seemed
to be pinstriped sports pads. Westwood said she'd been
inspired by Roman armour. The coat's references include
gladiator garb, motorcycle jackets, roller derby-uniforms. Mad
Max might have worn it to the office. When Acker moved, the
pads parted, revealing her tight and tattooed muscles. On the
bottom, she wore bondage pants.

She signed my copy of *Great Expectations*. "Love, Kathy."
I loved her books. I loved her clothes.

"Kathy had such élan, everything she touched was somehow made grander," Bellamy writes in "Digging Through Kathy's Stuff," her essay on Acker and Acker's clothes and the creation of "Kathy Forest."

Acker liked the outré, and designers who delivered it. Bellamy remembers her bedecked in a silver bodysuit "that looked like a prop from David Bowie's Ziggy Stardust tour, a tiny spacesuit." Remembers "Kathy holding court in a femmy short plaid dress, empire style, tight around her bust then flaring out. Some kind of frou-frou at the shoulders."

"Since no regular person would wear them," Bellamy writes, "could one say these clothes ever were in fashion?" She interviewed Kaucyila Brooke, a photographer who's documented over a hundred of Acker's outfits. Among them: a white hoedown dress. An orange suit with a holstein-patterned collar. Stirrup pants, and not only one pair. Acker, says Brooke, had a bit of Liberace about her. I wonder: did Kathy Acker and Dolly Parton go shopping together?

"She looked like a clown," Bellamy writes, "but a totally confident, powerful clown." Like Liberace, like Parton, like Prince—Acker created herself at least partly through clothing. "The gap between our intentions and the effects we create is what Diane Arbus ruthlessly brought into her photographs," Bellamy writes, "a gap, that whenever I recognize it, opens a pang of love in me. Kathy managed to create exactly the effect she intended, but her clownishness, her bald construction of a persona also opened that gap."

In winter of 2006, Bellamy dug out Acker's clothes. "On a shelf above our heads are stacked four large packing boxes," she writes. "The bottom one is labeled in black marker "Acker's Clothes" in Kathy's own handwriting. The boxes were packed by professional movers on the eve of her return from London in fall 1997."

The clothes are kept in Los Angeles, in the care of Acker's confidante and executor, Matias Viegener. "Once we get the boxes on the floor," Bellamy writes, "we start to rummage through them. Matias pulls out a black mass of fabric. 'This one's my favorite—I'll never get rid of it—because nobody has been able to figure out how you're supposed to wear it.'"

According to Viegener, Acker didn't take terribly good care of her clothes. Food stains them. Acker, he said, was a shopaholic. If she found something she liked, she'd take one in every colour. A black Gaultier dress grabbed Bellamy. It had a wool skirt with a diaphanous bodice. Sleeves of sheer mesh. A coat of arms embossed on the back. But whose family has such an insignia? In black flock, a consecration cross with 69 at its centre. Leaves sprout between the arms and neck of the cross. Lightning bolts blaze down either side. Scrolling over the cross, in faux-Gothic font: "Too Fast to Live, Too Young to Die."

The dress is from Gaultier's "Forbidden Gaultier" collection of 1987. I have a brooch from that show. It's steel, a British bobby's badge, a Brunswick star, with the same slogan stamped into it. I couldn't afford a dress. Gaultier winking at Westwood: Too Fast to Live, Too Young to Die was, for a while, the name of the shop that Westwood and Malcolm McLaren ran on Kings Road in London. Later, it was known as World's End. "Kathy often complained about not being famous enough," Bellamy tells me. "Like she thought fame was her due and she'd been cheated out of it. So dressing in this famous designer rock-and-roll costume-y way was, perhaps, a way of shouting out that fame persona."

"Kathy's Gaultier dress sits on my dresser, me on my bed writhing and grunting. It's as if the dress has consciousness, is waiting for something, as I come I hear something coming from the dresser, something faint, a rustle, a breath."

Bellamy took the dress home. Stared at it. Spoke to it. Had sex while it looked on. She wrote about it.

"Kathy's dress sits atop my dresser and I want to turn this dress into a doll, it would resonate with voodoo, would resonate with Kathy's stolen doll fucking passage, but the dress refuses to budge in that direction—the dress has presence, an aura, it sits there haughty as a popular girl who refuses to talk to me—stubbornly inanimate."

A kind of alchemy.

This is what Bellamy did so beautifully with the Gaultier dress, and with the garments in "Kathy Forest." She turned prêt-à-porter into ectoplasm.

"Ectoplasm, or teleplasm, as it is sometimes called," wrote séance investigator Julien J. Proskauer in *The Dead Do Not Talk*, "is a mysterious protoplasmic substance that streams out of the bodies of mediums. This is manipulated by the spirits in order that they may materialize; hence, in a sense, they use it to shape themselves into a corporeal form."

Acker wore her dresses, wore them out. Shaped them, and stained them: blood, sweat, supper stains. Bellamy didn't dry clean them. She hung them in an art gallery, where they seem spooky, spectral, signs from the afterlife. Like remainders from Acker's life, but also like Acker's doubles. Ectoplasm, according to occultists, is supposed to be the cloth from which the cosmos is cut—more substantial than matter itself. "Truly," said British spiritualist Oliver Lodge in 1925, "it may be called the living garment of God." What does it mean when God's garment is a Gaultier? Is Gaultier God? Is Kathy Acker?

Is the universe stretch velvet?

On the second night of the "Kathy Forest" show, Bellamy delivered a reading of "Digging Through Kathy's Stuff." "I wore an all-white outfit," Bellamy says, "because at the end of my talk I bring up an account of a reading Kathy gave of

Eurydice in the Underworld a few months before she died, where she was wearing all white.

"Right before I went to read," she says, "I went to the bathroom, and this day-old cut on my thumb that had scabbed over, broke open and a few drops of blood fell onto the outside of the pants, down by the crotch. The atmosphere of the reading was one of a ritualistic summoning of Kathy. So, of course it began with a spilling of blood."

A little of her lecture: "Kathy's outfit seems intrinsic to the experience. A slash of white in the darkness, she becomes an angel, Eurydice the death angel, her completely still body bleached in the darkness like a marble figure perched atop a tomb. When we transferred her ashes to the urn, ashy dust poofed into the air. All of us must have breathed it in."

"Towards the end of my reading," she tells me, "a huge cable fell from the ceiling of the auditorium and dropped right down into the audience in the form of a black noose. Everyone screamed and laughed. I had to wait quite a while for the audience to calm down to finish the reading. This convinced many that the clothes were haunted. After the reading some people were too spooked to go up and look at the clothes again, but most people raced upstairs.

"It was beautiful," Bellamy says of reaction to her show, "a pervasive sense of connection and awe." Some of the awe was amusing. "I was confronted with a lot of art patron types," she says to me, "mostly women, who wouldn't stop talking to me, and who could spot a Vivienne Westwood or Comme des Garçons from across the room. I would get asked questions, 'Where did she find a 'Vivvy' in San Francisco? I haven't been able to find one here.' It was all about shopping zeal and lusting after the clothes."

In "Digging Through Kathy's Stuff," Bellamy quotes a line from *A Discussion of Ghosts*, a Buddhist book: "Happy ghosts live pleasant lives full of good food and beautiful clothes."

The dead, like the living, crave nice clothes. Where does Kathy Acker's ghost shop? Are there ghost boutiques? Ghost couturiers? Charles Frederick Wraith? Boolenciaga? Do dead fashions have an afterlife?

Kathy Acker's ghost is in Westwood. Something from the "Pirates" show. She is made of ectoplasm, as are her clothes. She is the same as her clothes—it's an effect that she strove for in life, an effect that she's finally sewn up.

As Acker once wrote: "It was the days of ghosts. Still is."

And an Acker line I love: "I was in that store."

2006

WHAT WOULD WE WEAR IN BED?
An Interview with Edmund White

What should a couturier wear?

It's a question that Edmund White put to me during the course of this interview, and it's complicated.

A couturière can wear her own creations; a couturier depends on other designers for his clothes. If clothes make the man, then the man who makes clothes is expected to be perfect: businesslike and artistic, serious and frivolous, stylish and timeless.

What should a fashion writer wear? It's a problem that puzzles me, and so I asked him about it. In fashion, where presentation is paramount, a writer must mingle with some of the world's most spectacular peacocks. A writer's concern is stylish sentences, which can't be worn to fashion shows, unfortunately. What does fashion care for words?

White is hardly what I'd call a follower of fashion: he does not attend the shows, nor does he dress in designer fashions. He is, however, a voracious lover of culture who has befriended and profiled some of the great designers of the last decades. He is interested in the social conduct of the fashion world; indeed, he is interested of all sorts of social conduct, especially sex.

Since he began publishing in the early 1970s, White has put out novels, short stories and all manner of belles lettres. Many of them are classics: the coming-out novel 'A Boy's Own Story', the AIDS-inflected 'The Beautiful Room is Empty'. 'Genet: A Life', his

109

biography of Jean Genet, won a National Book Critics Circle award, and deservedly so. 'Hotel de Dream', a recent novel about Stephen Crane, is a jewel. What binds these disparate books together are his rich depictions of demimondes. This is among his strong suits, I'd say: writing about demimondes, about what happens when different demimondes meet and drink and fight and fuck. I pressed him for details of the fashion world and its denizens: how they get dressed and undressed.

I visited him at his apartment in New York City. I didn't know what to wear, so I wore jeans and took him lilies.

LA VIE EN ROBES

EW: I'm starting a memoir about Paris in the 1980s.

DM: I believe I first saw your work in an issue of *Vogue*; you were writing from Paris.

EW: When I was there I wrote for all the Condé Nast magazines, but mostly for *Vogue*. I think they gave me a monthly stipend, it was enough to pay the rent. The very first thing I did in Paris was write about why Americans like Proust so much. I can't remember my argument. It was totally made up.

(Laughter)

Then one of the first things I did was to interview Eric
Rohmer, and it was absolutely insane because my French
wasn't very good, but I lied about it and said that I spoke
perfect French. And so I could ask the questions, but I didn't
know what he was saying back. I couldn't ask follow-up
questions. As it turns out, he was saying these terribly
interesting things, because he was the most intellectual of all
French film directors. It was totally wasted on me.

DM: You covered fashion stories, too, didn't you?

EW: It was a big period for fashion. I think it was one of the
most fashion-conscious decades in the twentieth century, in
Paris, at least. It was the period of Christian Lacroix, which
was the last house of haute couture to open; and, of course, it's
closed already. I knew him and wrote the very first interview
with him—it was for *Vanity Fair*—and went to spend time
with him in Arles. That was the look for him the first year, the
look of Arles: all those big prints. He posed as a couture
person, but he was actually an art historian and had a PhD
from the University of Montpellier, and he was sort of from
that region but not really. The big takeaway phrase about him
was, "At last, a straight man designing clothes for women!"

But in fact he wasn't all that straight, though he did have a wife. They had lovers who were brothers of each other.

DM: You were friends with Yves Saint Laurent.

EW: Yves Saint Laurent was very drugged and drunk and just out of it. He was a fascinating man who could sort of get it together to produce these shows every year, and he probably had the best sense of colour of anybody in the twentieth century, he had an extraordinary eye for colour and for combinations of colour.

Azzedine Alaïa was my favorite, as a designer but mostly as a person. He was just totally charming and interesting and amusing from beginning to end. He's a little guy who lives about his shop, like a typical Arab—he literally lives above the space that holds his atelier and runway. There's a shop there, the runway, the atelier, and his living quarters, and the quarters of the girls he works with, they all live there.

He was very funny and very observant. He had very vivid memories of his childhood in Tunisia. They were kind of poor, and he remembered the once a month when Umm Kulthum would sing. She would sing, though nobody knew for how long she would sing. It was a certain day every month. His grandfather would send him to the local café at six in the morning to stand by the radio to save a place for him, which he would occupy until six in the evening. His grandfather would come, and the men would all put some jasmine behind his ears and they would be weeping as she would sing. This would go on for hours. He had total memories of that.

DM: How could he forget?

EW: One of the biggest problems that any couturier has is, What is he himself going to wear? Many of them go for this sort of business suit. That's wrong, too, because it looks so common. Savile Row, that's not right either. Azzedine's solution was to wear these black silk Chinese pajamas.

DM: They're his signature.

EW: Azzedine liked to work all night. I remember nights with him when he had the sixteen-year-old Naomi Campbell, who was a dream, so sweet—he'd have her on a dais, and he'd run around like Nebuchadnezzar with pins in his mouth, and he'd pin her together. He's called the architect of the body, and unlike Lacroix, who would sort of do a sketch with very little idea of how it would look on somebody, and who would hand it over to *les petites mains,* whose interpretations of the sketch was really half the work—Azzedine was really not like that, he'd do the whole thing himself on the body and relate it there, sort of like Balanchine, who'd say he created a ballet on a particular dancer.

THANK GOD FOR CHRISTIAN LACROIX

DM: As you mentioned, Lacroix was celebrated for his supposed straightness. It's often said that gay fashion designers don't know how to make women beautiful, or don't want to.

EW: The myth is that gay men are hostile to women and want to undermine them, want to flatten their breasts and put them in men's clothing and make them look ridiculous, want in every way to desexualize them and make them ugly. It's the gay male's revenge. It's a pre-1960s view of gay men, based on the idea that gay men were competing with women for men. It's crazy if you think about it. Gay men are in fashion to make *belles* frocks, to make women beautiful—and to make money. It shows the power of this myth, which used to be called Homintern—it was a term for a conspiracy cooked up by a secret society of gay men.

DM: I was terribly disappointed to find out that there wasn't a secret society. I had high hopes of controlling the world.

THE GAY CONSPIRACY, PART ONE

DM: When you were starting out as a writer in New York, what were gay men wearing?

EW: There was a dichotomy, it was man and boy. The boy was the object of desire. The boy was slender and starved himself. He wore black pegged pants, black shoes, a powder blue cashmere sweater and lots of perfume. He wore his hair long.

DM: He was Audrey Hepburn.

EW: This was even before the Beatles. It was okay to be twinky and feminine—he'd have one hand on his hip to excite the men. I straightened my hair to have a surfer look and starved myself a little to be thin. The ideal was the ephebe, it was important to look as much as an ephebe as possible. Of course this all came to a crashing end when you were thirty. At thirty, you were no longer attractive.

(Laughter)

DM: I really shouldn't laugh.

THE GAY CONSPIRACY, PART TWO

DM: How did you dress when you went to Paris?

EW: I was a Village bohemian who wore jeans with holes in
them and leather jackets and t-shirts. It's a very different set of
rules. In America, it was definitely the Village People look that
was considered hot. The hard hat, the jeans and leather vest.

I remember David Rieff—we were very close at that time, not
later—he told me that in Paris, just to go to buy a loaf of bread,
you had to put on a coat and tie, so you better change your
ways. I remember that was true, and I did change my ways. I
tried to dress nicely. I had just lost a lot of weight and I could
fit into nice clothes.

In America, the only sexy image for men is working-class men;
whereas that's not true in Europe. Businessmen, intellectuals
and professors, artists—all those people could be considered
sexy. The way that they dress, in jeans and sports jacket with
an open collar, could be considered hot. In America, the
working-class look was it. To some degree that was true in
England, but not at all in France or in the Latin world which is
what I know best. I don't really know the Protestant Europe.

(Laughter)

When I came back to New York for a brief holiday, there was a very hot gay guy living above me on Lafayette St. And I remember he said, "Oh, my God, you smell like cologne, that's so revolting; if there's one thing I hate, it's cologne on a man." And I thought, "Oh, boy, that takes me back." It took me back to the rules for getting into the Mineshaft: no cologne. Everybody was supposed to smell like old sweat. That was supposed to be hot.

(Laughter)

THE GAY CONSPIRACY, PART THREE

DM: Paris in the 1980s marked a very gay moment for fashion. There was Claude Montana, who had very S/M overtones. There was Jean Paul Gaultier, whose women's wear was often the same as his menswear.

EW: I can't say that gay people wore those clothes, at least not in Paris. In those years gay people there finally became identifiable as gay. They had never been so before. There'd been no gay ghetto, they had never been openly gay. Finally, a small percentage of them came out and became identifiable. They would wear these green nylon bomber jackets, jeans that were folded up at the bottom, orange work boots, shaved skulls; eventually there were tattoos and piercings.

DM: Was that adapted from a uniform of some sort, a working-class uniform, *à la* the skinheads?

EW: I don't know. People like Didier Lestrade, he pioneered that look. Intellectuals would dress that way. And then finally Guillaume Dustan—it's a pen name. He wrote a book, *Dans Ma Chambre*, I loved it. It was first-person *récit* about somebody who is living the gay life. He had a complete closet full of tit clamps and poppers and his boots and his whips. And *godemichés*—what do you call those? Dildos.

DM: I only have high-school French.

EW: He writes about all those things and in a scary way. I thought, this is so good. Either he's just a club kid himself and he'll never write another book, or he's a professor who's not at all like that and who's learned this from his boyfriend. So I invited him to tea. He showed up in jeans and guinea t-shirt and a black leather jacket that smelled and a shaved head. He was a judge in Polynesia. He had a broken arm because his boyfriend had just broken it.

DM: It happens.

EW: He went on to write many books and he started a publishing house. He was a great prophet of unsafe sex. He was always screaming at everyone to stop having safe sex. And he lived by his rules. And now he's dead. He was from a very bourgeois family and he had a chic little sister who worked a couple blocks away at 192 Books on 10th Avenue, which Paula Cooper runs, and who wore little Chanel suits and had a pearl necklace. That was his sister, that was the family he was from.

FASHION AND WRITING

DM: Fashion and writing—do you see any similarities between them?

EW: I don't think it's so different from painting, it's painting from fabric. And is painting like writing? I think so. I suppose in some ways it's a little more like high-quality journalism in the sense that it was meant to be ephemeral from the beginning. The French take it very seriously, they have not one but two museums of fashion, I think that somebody like Pierre Bergé is the ruling figure of French cultural life, in part because he's so generous and he's always investing in all things artistic. I think there's something venerable about fashion in France, it's been around a long time.

It's interesting, Parisians all have such contempt for American fashion, and they really think it's so pitiful. Azzedine came over here once and was taken through the Fashion Institute of Technology's collection of clothes, and on one side they had the European clothes and on one side, the American. And he wasn't really paying attention to the American side, until he saw this one dress, and he said, "I think that's on the wrong side, it's so good." And they said, "No, that's Charles James."

DM: Who's not really American.

EW: No, he's English, and very European.

DM: There's not very much good fashion literature.

EW: Very little.

DM: It's hard to capture the fashion world.

EW: People don't really know that world. And I'd say that most novelists are professors on little campuses somewhere; they don't seem to know much.

DM: There's Zola's novel, *The Ladies' Paradise*.

EW: *Le Bonheur des Dames*. I know it well. It ends with a great white sale!

DM: There's Mallarmé's writing on fashion, and there's Baudelaire.

EW: I would like to write a book about Baudelaire but nobody wants me to. I can't get anybody to commission me because nobody knows who he is in America.

DM: He had such an impact on how we think about perfume, jewelry, fashion.

EW: If you read the history of aesthetic ideas, it is the dullest thing ever written. All aesthetic ideas tend to be extremely conservative. There are very few ideas, really. Even if you read Santayana's *The Sense of Beauty*, or all these different people, they all say the same fucking thing, they repeat themselves endlessly, and they all say one thing and only one thing, which is, "Imitate nature." And, finally, you get Baudelaire, who says, "I despise nature and nothing is worse than a woman who's natural looking and women should look artificial and sick."

DM: That sounds like Homintern talk.

EW: The other person I think is kind of good is Anne Hollander, who was married to John Hollander, the poet, and now she's married to a philosopher, Thomas Nagel. She wrote a book called *Seeing Through Clothes*. Her theory in that is that when you see a nude painting, say, by Goya, what you're really seeing is a body that's been shaped and sculpted by the contemporary ideas of clothes; so, for instance, *La maja desnuda*, those Roma women have their breasts up high, in the same way that their bodices would raise the up, raise them up and suppress them; or when you see something like Lucas Cranach the Elder's Eve, she has these high breasts and this long sloping belly that seems to be the centre of erotic interest, and then these confused legs stuck on. And that seems to represent how the clothes of that time worked, because again they had these high little bodices and then this sloping long stomach, and then confusing-looking skirts where you couldn't see the legs.

DM: There's another side to that: if bodies are shaped by clothes, then clothes are also shaped by bodies. Clothes become relics. I'm thinking of Jacques Guerin, the perfumer, who was consumed by Proust and collected his clothing.

EW: Yes, I saw his collection. He was extremely rich and extremely nice. Well, he was nice to me. He had black servants whom he ridiculed openly. He was a bastard, as was his brother. So was Genet, whom he supported and took care of. So was Violette Leduc. This was what held them all together as a group. They made a silent film which has been lost. It involved a baptism, which is quite funny if you remember that they're all bastards. Genet was the baby, Violette Leduc was the nurse, Jacques Guerin's brother was the priest.

The weirdest case I ever heard about was Leon Edel, the biographer of Henry James. He would buy Henry James's underclothes at auction and he would wear them. And this was in Honolulu, where he lived!

WHAT WOULD WE DO IN BED?

DM: In your essay "The New Historical Novel," you write that "a lesser novelist attempts to make up for an insufficient grasp of the soul of an epoch by devoting himself or herself to its upholstery."

EW: Yes.

DM: In your historical novel *Fanny*, which follows Frances Trollope on her tour of the United States in the early 1800s, she sees American girls' dresses and sums them up as "common frocks." It's so understated.

EW: I don't think Trollope, the son, describes clothes that much; it is quite an interesting thing to describe, but only if the character herself would be noticing it.

DM: It's in contrast to the scene in *Hotel de Dream* in which Stephen Crane discovers drag queens at a bar in downtown New York. The description of the drag queens is detailed. You go to town on those girls.

EW: There's quite a bit of research about them. There was a raid on that bar that I describe. When I first came to New York, I would go to that bar without knowing that it was The Slide, and had been the first gay bar in NY. It was called the Bleecker St. Tavern at that time and it was around the corner from where I lived on MacDougal between Bleecker and Houston. We'd go there every night and it wasn't a gay bar. It had these rickety stairs that were condemned and had these rickety stairs leading up to a condemned balcony. We just never thought about it. The whole place was almost completely empty. There was this one very tired old waitress, very sweet, waiting on everybody. She had dyed black hair. She was probably a lesbian, she always seemed to perk up when we'd bring girls. It turned out that it was the very first gay bar, and now it's a rundown, awful place called Kenny's Hideaway. I was standing there one day on the sidewalk in front of it and I started talking to the owner of it. He said, "Yeah, come down with me and I'll show you downstairs, there are these little rooms where the prostitutes would take their customers." We went down there and we could see these little separate rooms.

DM: In gay culture, time is out of time. A writer could describe gay culture to the death and not capture the greater culture at all.

EW: It's like black culture would be.

DM: It has to be described; you have to describe it.

EW: It's so different from ours, that's partly what fascinated me. Even when I was a boy in the 1950s, the whole idea was to get trade, straight trade, and then if they got mean and beat you up, then you'd say, "My trade turned dirt." It was assumed that no gay person would want to have sex with another gay person. People would say, "What would we do, bump pussies?" That was the thing to say. "What on earth would we do in bed?"

THE PINK BLACK PANTHER

DM: You're preppy.

EW: (Chuckles)

DM: I associate you with a certain classic American style. When I see you, you're often in navy blazers and chinos, or in jeans and a t-shirt, as you are today.

EW: Well, I went to a prep school. I'm very middle class that way. My idea would be to blend into the background. I don't really want to be noticeable.

DM: William Burroughs said that the best thing was not to be noticed, that the best way to operate in our culture was to blend in. Though he hardly blended in: his suit and tie became a signature style.

EW: Certainly writers want to blend in. I believe especially that after a certain age you long for anonymity. Unless you're Quentin Crisp. Jean Genet felt that you couldn't be effeminate after thirty without risking ridicule. You had to turn yourself into something butch after thirty if you were going to survive as a sexual being, or even as a social being. So he did this major operation on himself. He butched himself up: his clothes, his manner. He shaved his skull. Genet was a tough guy; I think he tried to look tougher than he really was.

DM: Which a lot of gay guys do.

EW: Genet had had long hair and been a prostitute, pretty much a feminine prostitute when he was very young. But sometimes when he would take lots of Nembutals, which he took every night, eight or nine of them, he would revert to his feminine side and would wear a pink nightgown and dance for the Black Panthers. Even in his sixties he would do this. I met a straight French photographer who had followed Genet around in America. He said, "I don't want to talk about that guy." I said, "Why not?" "Oh," he said, "he was my hero but he disappointed me. If you must know: he'd put on a fucking nightgown and dance for the Panthers." I thought, this can't be true, Genet was so careful about being butch. A year went by and I thought this photographer was just making up shit. And then I interviewed Angela Davis, and she said, "Oh, Genet, he was a great man, he was the original gender bender, I remember when he'd wear a pink nightgown and he'd dance."

2013

I WAS MISS GENERAL IDEA

I was Miss General Idea.

If this doesn't surprise you, it should: my name doesn't appear anywhere in "Haute Culture," the General Idea retrospective that opened at the Art Gallery of Ontario last week.

I may not be in "Haute Culture," but Miss General Idea sure is. She's a character, a conceptual caprice. Jorge Zontal, Felix Partz and A.A. Bronson—the three Toronto artists that comprised the General Idea collective—created her in the late 1960s, and she flits through the following fifteen years' worth of their work.

General Idea were Warhol's Canadian cousins, making art, magazines and installations that mocked and mimicked the machinery of stardom. Miss General Idea was the brightest star in their sky from the moment she was conceived until the mid-1980s. She was the beauty queen to end all beauty queens, a parody of Miss America and other pageant glamourpusses.

Miss General Idea was a figure as real as any beauty queen; that is, not real at all. Through her, the artists in General Idea were able to plunge themselves into an aspect of stardom that they loved and loathed: glamour. They designed a boudoir for her. They drew up plans for a pavilion that would be built in her honour. They held pageants in which men and women would win her title, at least for a time.

In 1971, General Idea created an "artist's conception" of her: a silkscreen on rubber of a woman—at least I think it's a woman—in a skirt, killer heels and what looks to be a black rubber bodysuit. "Haute Culture" at the AGO includes many more of her looks. There's the 1940s style dress that was worn by Miss General Idea Pageant participants in 1971. There's the VB dress of 1975, which consists of three Robert Smithson-y pyramids—a hat, a blouse and a skirt—that are constructed from venetian blinds.

General Idea generated glamour in order to parody it; the artists inhabited the world of fashion in order to fuck with fashion. Of course, being fashionable complicated their critique of fashion: was the critique for real, or were they simply co-opting criticism for fashion, furthering fashion's reach? Miss General Idea embodied this ambiguity; she made fashion seem as complex and intellectual as I always wanted it to be.

Which is why I stepped into her stilettos. In 1985, I proclaimed myself Miss General Idea. I had to: she wasn't real, and I needed her to be.

In 1985, I went to the Art Gallery of Ontario to see a survey show of General Idea's work. I was sixteen. I had heard of the artists, but not of Miss General Idea.

I was smitten. She was a creature of glamour, and for me glamour was a synonym for fashion, and fashion was a synonym for gay. Her duties: perverting and playing with beauty, fame and sexuality.

These were duties that I knew I could discharge. She was the ambassadress of artificiality and abasement; I was a spotty teen who longed for glamour and wanted badly to be abased. She wasn't real, nor was I.

I crowned myself. Then I bused back to my hometown of Peterborough, Ontario. I did my best to embody the title. I was faggy. I was condescending. With a friend, I published a zine, *The Aquamarine Poodle*. The title was inspired by a triad of poodles—one pink, one gold, one aquamarine—that appeared in a number of General Idea's pieces. More often than not, the poodles were engaged in a ménage à trois.

My friend and I sold our zine in the school cafeteria. It included my reviews of the recent prêt-a-porter shows in Paris. I hadn't been in Paris for the shows, but that didn't stop me. I also penned an essay about Paris. I tried to simulate the style of General Idea's writings, which parroted and parodied the academic-ese of *Artforum* and blended it with the bon mots of Diana Vreeland's *Vogue*: "Have you ever been to Paris?" I wrote. "Paris is an object, a 20th century icon imbued with the trappings of glamour, its characteristics and gestures." It goes on and on. I discuss image and violence and surveillance. I couldn't dress up in Miss General Idea's garments, so I tried a different kind of drag: words.

I lost myself in Miss General Idea. What I didn't grasp was that she was already lost.

"Miss General Idea has fled." So wrote General Idea in 1984. The artists said she had abandoned them; in truth, they had abandoned her. She had amused them, but she was no longer their muse. They had turned their attention to other matters; for a while, it was the media and TV; then it was AIDS. In 1994, both Partz and Zontal died of AIDS-related illnesses; General Idea was lost, too.

"Haute Culture," the AGO's current retrospective, has impressive pieces from what A.A. Bronson, the sole survivor of the group, calls "The AIDS Era." There's lots of General Idea's great early work. There are architectural plans for the 1984 Miss General Idea Pavillion. There are relics from the ruins of the pavilion, which burned down in 1977 (it didn't really burn down, since it was never really built: the pavilion was a ruse, as were the relics). There are oodles of fucking poodles. It's all fun, all fancifully perverse, though the later AIDS art casts a long shadow on it. The mirrored surface of Felix Part's big Mylar handbag (1968) is reflected by the mirrored surfaces of the pill-shaped Mylar balloons of "Magi© Bullet" (1992). From purse to prescription: General Idea reflected the fashion world, the art world, the gay world, and their mirrors mirrored me mirroring their mirrors.

2011

THE BLITZ KID

Fashion or faggotry—I don't know which found me first.

I've always loved fashion and I've always been a faggot. I'm never comfortable in bars or clubs and I've never been to a backroom or a bathhouse. Boutiques are my backrooms.

The best boutiques I've been in? There was World's End in London, where I first saw a Vivienne Westwood; there was If Boutique in New York City, where I first felt a Jean Paul Gaultier; there was the Holt Renfrew in Toronto, where I fell for an early collection by Maison Martin Margiela.

There was Seesaw. Seesaw was in Toronto; it's where I saw Blitz. Blitz wasn't a big label, but it was big for me, because Carole Pope wore it.

"With its visual flair and its peculiar brand of rock," a magazine said in 1982, "Rough Trade, judged both by sight and sound, is the most distinctive act in Canadian show business."

Rough Trade was founded in the 1970s, but found fame during the New Wave days of the 1980s. Though the band had numerous members through the years, the core stayed the same: Kevan Staples wrote and played the music; Pope wrote the words and sang.

I liked her style, though I'd be hard pressed to describe it.

She wore safety pins and bondage gear, but she wasn't punk;

she wore severe, sharp-shouldered suits, but she wasn't New Wave.

Punk, New Wave, New Romanticism—she flirted with these looks, but they didn't fit her. She was something else. She was gay—butch as hell, singing songs about dykes and queens and some "trade who turned tricks in latrines." She was fashionable—she worshipped and wore the designers of the day, and she wrote about them in the song "Fashion Victim": "Montana, Fendi, Lagerfeld," she sang, "Mugler, Kenzo, Chloe."

Pope was the first singer I saw who loved labels. She confirmed a feeling that I'd from an early age: gays were made for fashion, and fashion was made for gays.

Carole Pope was my first favourite singer. I was a fan of hers in a way that I hadn't been a fan of anybody's before. I wanted to look like her. I wanted to talk like her. I wanted to know her. I came close. I interviewed her once—a local radio station put me in touch with her so that I could talk to her by telephone for a class project.

It was 1981. I was twelve.

"What do you do during the day?" I asked.

"I lie around a lot, I shop," she said. "I'm in my pyjamas."

"Where do you shop?"

"I like shopping in New York. That's where you can get the really great clothes. I like to shop in Toronto, too, there are amazing designers here."

"What does Rough Trade mean?"

"Do you know anything about gay slang? I like reading about old gay slang and outdated slang. Rough trade was what you called a tough male prostitute, a trick that you picked up for rough sex."

I was too titillated to reply.

It's not that she made me realize I was gay; I knew it already. It's not that she made it okay for me to be gay; I knew it was okay. She made me realize what kind of gay I was, or wanted to be: fashionable, a "victim of fashion," as she sang, "fashion and accessories."

Avoid Freud (1980) was my introduction to Rough Trade. It was the band's second album; it was its first hit.

I played and played it. It was her voice – I wasn't sure if she was a man or a woman. It was her look – I wasn't sure if she was a man or woman.

It was the lyrics: there was fashion, there was fucking.

At the Junos, a national music award show, Rough Trade performed its hit, "High School Confidential." When Pope sang the line "she makes me cream my jeans when she comes my way," she clutched her crotch. She was in all in red—red leather pants and a red leather blazer.

I was watching it on live TV. I loved it.

In 1981, Rough Trade released another album, *For Those Who Think Young*. At the same award show that year, Anne Murray won Best Female Vocalist; Pope accepted it on her behalf. She was wearing leather: a button-up coat sewn of bars of red and black suede with shoulder pads that would make Mugler blush.

Where did clothes like that come from?

When Rough Trade toured to my hometown—a city an hour or so away from Toronto—I was in the front row.

I remember Pope pretended to masturbate with her microphone stand. I remember she mock-masturbated with her hand, too, then sniffed it.

I remember she was wearing white—white baggy pants with a white unconstructed blazer. It was the same outfit she was wearing on the cover of *For Those Who Think Young*.

In the liner notes to the album, she credited her clothes to Blitz, and thanked Marilyn Kiewiet, the label's designer. In the liner notes to *Shaking the Foundations* (1982), she thanked Kiewiet again; she also thanked Seesaw, a shop in Toronto. I traveled there as soon as I was able to and bought a sweater. Blitz made it. What did it make me?

Seesaw was a shoebox of a store in a shopping arcade.

It looked like many stores I'd been in, but with better clothes. The labels were Japanese, German, Spanish. There were labels I couldn't identify.

There was Blitz. The Fall/Winter collection was on the racks. The sweater I picked up looked a little like the coat Carole Pope wore. It was double-breasted with a flap that came down across the front. It was black with red stripes and squiggles. It was on sale: $120.

When I slipped it on, I became—who? I became Carole Pope. I became Kevan Staples. I became somebody who might be in Rough Trade's world: an artist, a fashion designer, a makeup artist or hairstylist. I wanted into Rough Trade's world; I thought that Seesaw was a way in, I thought that a sweater was a way in, I thought that shopping was a way in. I thought: If only I have the right things to wear.

Born in Britain, Pope came to Canada with her family as a kid. She attended high school in Scarborough—the "depths of Scarborough," as she said in her memoir, *Anti-Diva*.

When she was done, she drifted downtown, to Yorkville. The city's music scene was centred there then. She played coffeehouses and bars with Kevan Staples. They called themselves O, after *The Story of O*. Then they became the Bullwhip Brothers.

Then, Rough Trade.

"Before she started earning much money, Pope shopped for striking second-hand styles at Amelia Earhart," the *Toronto Star* reported in 1984. "Her few designer creations were made by Sandy Stagg, who used to own and design for Amelia Earhart."

In the 1970s, Sandy Stagg specialized in stocking styles from the 1930s and 1940s; her own designs were inspired by those decades. She was a doyenne of the downtown scene: what she wore and said was news. She was written up often in *FILE Megazine*, the magazine put out by General Idea. She appeared on the cover of *FILE*'s "Glamour Issue" in 1975, or at least her leg did. It was wearing the Miss General Idea shoe.

Miss General Idea was a character, a conceptual caprice. General Idea created her as a parody of Miss America and Miss World. They put on pageants in which men and women would win her title. Staged at the Art Gallery of Ontario, The Miss General Idea Pageant of 1975 featured performances by Rough Trade. The band performed numbers they'd selected specially for the night—there was "I Like It, but Is It Art?" which included the lyric: "Sylvia Plath getting gassed, Warhol getting shot by Solanas, I like it, I like it, I like it, but is it art?" There was "Beauty Queen," which included the line: "You're not a drag queen or a dinge queen or a rice queen or a dairy queen ...."

Then came punk.

Pope put a shock of purple in her hair. She wore pants with see-through plastic windows sewn into the seat. She and the band performed *Restless Underwear*, a musical revue co-starring Divine, in New York and Toronto. Pope was in a vinyl bondage suit.

When Rough Trade toured, they'd take in Fiorucci and Maxfield's. In Paris, Pope, Staples and Kiewiet found Claude Montana's leather factory and stocked up on samples. If the pieces they wanted were too pricey to purchase, Kiewiet simply made them – she had a studio, and she had skills; she'd apprenticed at a leather goods firm in Amsterdam that created coats, she said, for every gambler and gangster in town.

When Seesaw started stocking Kansai, Pope started wearing it. Kansai Yamamoto had been a fashion star since he showed in London in 1971. He was best known for costuming David Bowie during his Ziggy Stardust and Aladdin Sane days. When he staged runway shows in Japan, the press said, he did it in stadiums—he had become a rock star himself. His clothing had a futuristic feel, sort of sci-fi meets Hokusai: there were contemporary silhouettes with cuts that recalled kimonos; they were splashed with Japanese characters and prints of waves or tigers. Pope bought a lot of it—in 1983, the style section of a Toronto newspaper stated that she was at risk of losing her style status if she didn't stop wearing it all the time.

I was shocked.

I was shocked by the editorial, shocked to think that Carole Pope wasn't fashionable.

She had been a model to me; more than fashionable, she'd seemed to be a spokesperson for fashion itself.

Then things changed. I'd discovered Jean Paul Gaultier; he seemed to render Montana and Mugler redundant. I'd seen Comme des Garçons and Yohji Yamamoto's clothes in *Vogue*; they made all the clothes I'd ever seen seem redundant.

Rough Trade broke up in 1988, though it seemed as if they'd broken up before that: *O, Tempora! O, Mores!* (1984) was the band's final studio album.

Seesaw closed up sometime after that. I didn't notice. Whenever I was in Toronto, I haunted a boutique on Bloor Street West that sold Gaultier for men. I loved the rubberized shirts, the pinstripe suits with bare backs, the skirts that were designed for men to wear. I can't recall the name of the boutique.

It will come to me.

2017

THAT STRANGE THOUGHT
An Interview with David Livingstone

What is fashion writing for?

"What is any writing for?" David Livingstone says. "If it's interesting, if it's done in an interesting way, then people will read it."

I asked David Livingstone what fashion writing is for because I wonder about it, and because he's the best fashion writer that Canada's ever had.

"People aren't naked," he says. "There's always something to say about colour, shape, texture. I like to stare at people. The only people I can get to stare back at me these days are infants."

David Livingstone is fast, funny, and—in real life, anyway—lewd. He's also smart, book smart, the best sort of smart. He knows what's new in fashion and he knows what was new way back when.

"There's a sad sort of glimmer of something," he says of fashion writing. "It's a flicker; it knows that it can never capture what it wants to capture, that it's always already gone."

I interviewed him about his writing and about writing about fashion. He smoked and talked to me about his career, from his days at the 'Globe and Mail' to his current role as editor-in-chief of 'Men's FASHION' magazine. I've been writing articles for David for over a decade. He's a daunting editor—I have no doubt that he could write any article I've done better than I did it. He's also a dear—he's groomed a generation of writers and photographers, from Sheila Heti to Bruce LaBruce.

1.

DM: I'm a fan.

DL: Oh, stop it.

DM: It's true. I think you're a great fashion writer, a great writer.

DL: Ladies and gentlemen, get out your designer hankies out, we're having a moment.

DM: When I was a teenager, I'd clip all of your stories and store them in a box beneath my bed. I wish I still had them.

DL: I still have them!

DM: You've kept everything you've done?

DL: I don't think so. I don't know anymore. I've got piles of shit everywhere—and some of it is my own. (laugh) I really should get it all organized. I need a librarian. I need a librarian to clean it all. The nicotine is on it almost like marmalade. (laugh)

2.

DM: Did you always dream of being a writer?

DL: No, no.

DM: OK, so when did you decide that?

DL: I didn't know you were supposed to want to be something. I'm still not sure. What's the point?

DM: There was a point then, maybe.

DL: Maybe. I studied English at the University of Toronto, and why did I do that? I liked it, and sort of did all right at it in high school. When I left university, that's when I started to write. Writing was never something that I had a mission for. I always imagined that if you wrote about things in a newspaper or anywhere, that you always knew every single thing about that. I just assumed! That is that old-fashioned, sort of, whatever, respect for a page with words on it. Fuck!

DM: I have a constant fear of not knowing enough.

DL: It's part of being a writer. On one hand there's the language, and then there's the thing of giving someone something amusing to read. Or amuse yourself. Or something!

3.

DM: When did you start writing for *FASHION*?

DL: I started writing for it in 1978, 1979.

DM: What were you covering?

DL: What was different then was that stories weren't offered by a certain company. I'd do profiles of designers in New York: Mary McFadden, Oscar de la Renta, Perry Ellis. Essentially that's what it was: profiles. I'd do Diana Vreeland and Richard Avedon. Iona Monahan, the fashion editor from Montreal. Do you know who that is?

DM: No.

DL: You don't know Iona Monahan?

DM: I don't.

DL: Iona got the Order of Canada before Jeanne Beker.

DM: (laugh)

DL: I wrote a profile of her. She was the canniest operator—she met me in Montreal for a first face-to-face interview, but then declined to participate after that. If Rufus Wainwright wants to do another opera, he should make it about her.

DM: A colourful figure?

DL: Fascinating. Irish from some poor suburb of Montreal. She designed the fashion show at Expo '67. Known for her great big glasses, known for hiring limos to bring her subjects, known for doing things with a certain whatever. Always wore black. Always went to Paris, never went to Milan. One season word came through that one of her daughters had murdered the other one in a fight over a pair of ski pants.

4.

DM: When you started at *FASHION*, what was happening in Toronto?

DL: Well, there was punk and new wave. That was the fun part of covering fashion and music at the same time. That was probably the greatest meeting of fashion and music I've ever seen.

DM: I remember Atomic Age.

DL: Atomic Age was important. It had early Vivienne Westwood. I remember little rubber penis-shaped buttons on white terry cloth.

DM: It's remembered it as *the* place where punk and fashion collided.

DL: Yes. Ruth Ann Lockhart and Rick Lockhart both came from Atomic Age, one going on to Holt Renfrew and the other to The Bay. There were things happening all over town back then. Carole Pope wore Blitz by Marilyn Kiewiet, the partner of Kevan Staples. Leighton Barrett. Clotheslines. Parachute. Not punk, but.

DM: I remember Leighton Barrett. I remember seeing him in a classic preppy sweater with a dog collar. It made quite an impression.

DL: I almost wore one today. And I might as well have.

DM: And General Idea.

DL: General idea goes back to the seventies. Looking at some of the photography in *WORN*, one is reminded somehow of *FILE* and General Idea.

DM: That's a high compliment.

DL: It should be.

5.

DM: When did you go to the *Globe and Mail*?

DL: In 1983. The first year that I did the collections in London, Paris and Milan would have been…'84? I don't know. I remember though the first season I was in Paris, I did interviews with Rei Kawakubo, Karl Lagerfeld, Claude Montana and—who was the other one? Gaultier.

DM: Intimidating!

DL: I was foolish. I mean I can remember preparing for my interview with Montana. I decided that I should conduct it completely in French.

DM: Did he reply in English?

DL: Yeah.

DM: I saw a recent interview with him.

DL: After the death of Wallis Franken, he was really beaten up in the press. Did you see a documentary that covered any of that?

DM: No. It was a short clip of him discussing an artist he admired. It was shocking because there's just so much cosmetic surgery and so much—cosmetics!

DL: But still in the same bomber, still the same hairstyle. There were rumours that he didn't wear one bomber, there was a bomber underneath the other bomber. Those shoulders didn't come with just one jacket.

DM: There were three titans at that time in Paris—Montana, Mugler, and Gaultier. Gaultier is, I suppose, the only one still in the spotlight.

DL: When I started, Gaultier was the show in Paris. Gaultier had the only evening show, at that time, too. He was special, those were special. It's interesting that even after that retrospective, the show that was in Montreal, which was quite amusing, even after that there's been no revival. What did he do wrong? I don't know. He stuck with that blond hair is what he did wrong.

6.

DM: What about Kawakubo?

DL: It would blow your mind.

DM: Was she a star when you first saw her show?

DL: I was lucky. My first encounter with Comme des Garçons was at a menswear show presented by the Designers Collective in New York. It would've been the early 1980s. Iona and I were the only ones onto it then.

DM: What was new about her menswear?

DL: The black. The interesting cut of the jackets. I had a white poplin shirt with a silver lamé collar. I felt as if I should be playing an accordion when I wore it.

DM: (laugh)

DL: I never saw a Comme des Garçons collection on the runway without going backstage for what we call a "go-see." I'd see the clothing in person and have a chat with Kawakubo.

DM: What is she like?

DL: She was stern. So am I. (laugh) Someone once told me that everything with her comes from great pain—I don't think anything with her is easy.

DM: She seems to speak in a clipped poetry.

DL: I always spoke to her through a translator. But yes, she says a lot in very few words. I don't know if they were always issued as official show notes but each collection came accompanied by a couple of words that summed up the show. It's interesting, whatever you'd call it, that "red is the new black," or "red is black," as a construction, it's hers. She started that. And it's not simply the language—there is a thought in that, and even as widespread as that construction became, there's still an echo of that strange thought. It's that way with Kawakubo, to go from her notes for a season into... what?

7.

DM: When did you start editing *Men's FASHION*?

DL: I started at around the same time that brightly-coloured socks came back into style for men. When was that—2010?

DM: You hadn't helmed a men's magazine before that?

DL: I'd been writing about menswear all along the way. I was once asked by a PR person who the magazine was aimed at. "Anybody who can read!" I said.

DM: There are things that you're supposed to write about at a men's magazine, though.

DL: Cars. Watches. The mix is changing a little—décor is something that men's magazines can do. It's fun—it's a smaller alphabet at a men's magazine but I enjoy it. It's all the same in the end anyway—men and women are interested in clothes.

DM: When the Gaultier exhibit was on in Montreal, you mentioned to me that it bothers you how poorly menswear is represented in terms of museum exhibitions and catalogues.

DL: The menswear was there, I think it was, a little bit, at that show. But generally speaking, it's absent.

DM: Why, though? Why do you think menswear is so poorly represented?

DL: I guess it's all about that whole thing that "real men don't think about fashion." It would all have to be that, it would.

DM: But don't gay men and women think about men's fashion? Or do women not think about men's fashion?

DL: At this point, no. What's being denied, really? What?

DM: I would think that museum curators would compensate for this.

DL: Where it was most noticeably absent was in the Alexander McQueen show at the Met. It was a very successful presentation, which made it very hard to argue with. But it would have been interesting to put in at least the first few men's shows. Those were important shows. I've never seen Yves Saint Laurent's men's collections exhibited.

DM: When I think of Saint Laurent menswear, I only think of what he wore.

DL: I don't know how many collections there were, or what that history was, but I'd love to know. Because that really was something, that jacket, those pants, that whole deal. With these two Saint Laurent movies coming out, and being with a men's magazine, I would like to do something on the history of Saint Laurent menswear. But I don't know where to start on that. Maybe a letter to Pierre Bergé, something. He must have a sense of that. And just what Helmut Berger wore, whatever he wore.

8.

DM: Why write fashion?

D: What do you mean?

DM: Does it matter to fashion designers?

DL: I think so. They like to read about themselves. It's funny, though, that you get no response for anything anyway, at least not from the people you write about.

DM: There must have been a few people who responded?

DL: Well, no, and yes, whatever. A letter here and there, a phone call. A beautiful letter from Kennedy Fraser. A nice note from Vivienne Westwood. Lovely notes from Geoffrey Beene.

DM: Would it be fair to say that Kennedy Fraser is your favourite fashion writer?

DL: Kennedy Fraser would be right up there. I interviewed her when she was at the *New Yorker*. I didn't know, actually, whether Kennedy Fraser was male or female.

DM: I've always presumed it's a woman.

DL: I didn't presume.

DM: Wise. Holly Brubach was the *New Yorker*'s fashion writer when I began to read the *New Yorker*.

DL: Yes, I was in touch with her in the last twelve months to see if she'd write a piece about golf, because she's really interested in golf.

DM: She used to have that Canadian connection—she did work for Birks?

DL: Yeah, weird. It was weird because before that it was Prada. Interesting career, interesting body of work in terms of what she knows about, because she knows a lot about golf and fashion and transgender issues and ballet. She did something, did she not, about that ballerina? You know the one? Who got taken down by polio? Tanaquil LaClerque. They were friends for the last several years of her life.

DM: I was introduced to another great *New Yorker* fashion writer, Lois Long, through an article you wrote in *The Look*.

DL: Lois Long, interesting figure in the history of fashion—of New York! She was at the *New Yorker* for a long time, from the 1920s.

DM: She was Lipstick.

DL: Yes, before she wrote under that name for a period. Before she was a writer, she was a figure about town, an icon of flapperdom or flapperhood. She was considered the New Woman in the 1920s.

DM: I had to dig up her articles on microfiche. They're completely uncollected.

DL: I'm glad I did that piece on her. I've got a box—not that I found a lot of material, but what I found is all gathered in a box. Her granddaughter happened to be living in Toronto, so at that point I met the daughter, Lois Long's daughter, at some apartment over on Queen Street West where they had been living upstairs. Lois Long's daughter with Peter Arno.

9.

DM: What about contemporary fashion writing?

DL: Lynn Yaeger. Judith Thurman. I bought a book of hers, *Cleopatra's Nose*, the other day. Alison Adburgham, the British writer who wrote the history of fashion in *Punch* and the biography of Liberty. She was a lovely writer. Sarah Mower is a great writer, I'd say. And Guy Trebay. There's nobody like him around. I could say that there's nobody else around at all!

DM: Do you read blogs?

DL: There was a moment where I was kind of interested in Tavi, what's her name, because it was kind of distinctive age-wise and point of view-wise really. Nathalie Atkinson does a good job, Nathalie does a great job in terms of stirring the pot and keeping the subject interesting.

DM: Yeah, she does her work, she works hard.

DL: And she goes out of her way somehow to avoid the conventional, in other words what we call "the news."

DM: Where does that instinct come from in you, the instinct to avoid the conventional?

DL: Nosiness!

DM: And shit disturbing, there must be some of that.

DL: Well, no, not really.

DM: Oh, you should see the angelic look I'm getting here.

DL: No! Oh fuck, if I wanted to be a shit disturber, there would be shit.

10.

DM: Do you still find pleasure in writing?

DL: Some. I've got curiosity on my side. After all these years it comes automatically. Bad habits probably, that's what you get! Just a lot of bad habits!

DM: I'm just so impressed you still have curiosity.

DL: Yeah, and more now than ever, because there's less known, less said, less information, for all the information that's given us.

DM: Since I got cancer it has been difficult to be as curious as I once was.

DL: Wouldn't that make you even more curious?

DM: I wish it did. See, that's the difference between us, look at you!

DL: What am I curious about? I'd start with, "Why me?" I'm curious about that. And, "What is this shit?" I'm curious about that. "When will it end?" I'm curious about that. And then there are all the other things that are worse. That's the great body of knowledge to accumulate: the things that are worse than this thing.

2014

SPANGLE IS A SYNONYM FOR SEQUIN

Codex Atlanticus.

The name of one of Leonardo da Vinci's notebooks. It's full of ideas for inventions. My favourite: a machine for making sequins.

It's a mess of pulleys and levers. A sheet of gold slides onto a table. Punch presses punch. Sequins drop into a basket below. Scrap gold slides out.

Or something like that. It was never actually built. Still, I have to mention it. There are few visionaries in the history of sequins. Leonardo's one.

Herbert Lieberman. He's another.

Strippers. Shriners. Sonja Henie.

Mr. Lieberman costumed them all. He sewed sequin headdresses. Ringling Bros. Circus ordered them. For elephants.

Mr. Lieberman manufactured sequins. His former factory in New York turned out six million spangles a day. Spangle is a synonym for sequin.

He pioneered sequin production in the United States. He pioneered the use of plastics in sequins. He invented a new species of sequin. By solving a problem that plagued plastic sequins. The problem: dirt. He invented the washable sequin.

I phone him at his home in Florida. To talk sequins. The history of. The making of. How he made sequin history.

"My father was an artist," Mr. Lieberman says. "He made the pennants they bring to college football games. In those days they were hand-painted." The 1910s. His father a teen.

"The company my father worked for started to embroider pennants," he says. "They taught my father the embroidery trade." Mr. Lieberman, Sr. struck out on his own. As the Algy Trimming Company. He did contract work. Embroidering fine ladies' wear.

"Then they found King Tut's tomb." Tutmania took America. Fashion designers designed sandals with Isis buckles. A "Luxor" gown in Egyptian colours. Gold and black. A New York City store advertised an Egyptian winter coat with "aristocratic" collar. The collar was squirrel.

Embroidery business boomed. Algy embroidered dresses with Egyptian motifs. Sphinxes. Scarabs. Hieroglyphics were big. It didn't matter what they meant. "My father did well," Mr. Lieberman says. "We always do well on fads. Who's that woman that's been married ten times? She played that queen? Elizabeth Taylor?" He laughs. "We sold more Cleopatra costumes."

King Tut wore sequins.

At least his mummy did. "When they found King Tut's tomb," Mr. Lieberman says, "everything was gold."

Gold sequins tucked between Tut's bandages. In the antechamber of the tomb lay a shirt. Shimmering with sequins. So Tut could dress well in the afterworld.

"Ornate gold rolled thin and cut out and hung on," he says. Egyptians glazed the gold. To stop scratches and chips. "Those were the first sequins."

The Roma migrated to Europe in the Middle Ages.

Dark hair. Dark eyes. The Roma hailed from India. Europeans mistook them for Egyptians. Called them Gypsies.

The Roma wore sequins. On belts. On blouses. "Gypsy coins," Mr. Lieberman says. "They came to be known as Gypsy coins. And it was real gold, authentic gold."

Europeans hated Gypsies. Loved Gypsy coins. King Charles VI of France hired a gold beater. To beat sequins. A French sumptuary law of 1294 declared that only royal princes could wear spangled embroidery.

Almanach des fabricans travaillant au matieres, d'or, argent, et autre metaux.

A directory published in Paris in 1810. It included a list of working goldsmiths. Almost a thousand. Among the smiths: "Manufacturers of spangles."

Their days were numbered. Napoleon and his army had just crawled back from Egypt. He'd tried to colonize it. Failed. His troops were weak. He'd fed them a new food supplement: gelatin.

Gelatin comes from carcasses. Boil cows. Horses. Old shoes work, too. Jelly rises up—this is gelatin. Napoleon hoped it would take care of his army's dietary needs. He was wrong. It's pure protein. No vitamins. It had other uses.

"The first form of plastic was gelatin," Mr. Lieberman says. France used gelatin in its paper money. Photographers used to develop photos on silver plates. Gelatin plates coated in silver worked just as well, they found.

And dress designers. They found that gelatin could be rolled into sheets, punch pressed, electroplated.

Voilà!—sequins.

"During the Great Depression," says Mr. Lieberman, "people were honest."

A customer owed Algy a debt of one hundred and seventy-five dollars. The customer had no cash. He had something else. Mr. Lieberman, Sr. got paid in sequins.

"It took two taxis to transport them," Mr. Lieberman says.

The sequins were gelatin. Made in Austria. Austria, Czechoslovakia—these were the capitals of sequin production. "And the colours," he says. "Vivid." The dye had lead in it.

"Gelatin melted if it got too hot," he says. Forget dry

cleaning. Forget ironing. "Someone would leave a garment close to the heating stove, it would melt." Moisture was no better. "Someone got caught in a rainstorm, it would melt." Washing machines liquefied sequins. "The early sequins you couldn't do anything with," he says. "They just looked beautiful. You could only sponge the garment a little to get the perspiration odor out."

Algy sequined nightclub dancers. Mardi Gras paraders. Sonja Henie wore Algy in her Hollywood Ice Revue. The first touring figure skating show. The first skater to sport sequins.

"My father taught himself how to stitch sequins," Mr. Lieberman says. "And he was quite successful. If people needed sequins, they looked to him to get it."

Then sequins vanished. "All the European supplies dried up in World War Two," Mr. Lieberman says. He himself served overseas. In Italy. A volunteer. His father persevered. "He had to learn how to manufacture sequins himself."

Algy tried a new plastic. "Eastman Kodak was producing acetate for their film stock," he says. "Clear plastic. They plated it on one side with real silver." Kodak customized acetate for Algy. "They coated the silver with a clear ink of the colour we desired. They coloured the other side as well."

The effect was brilliant. "The light would penetrate through the colour, hit the silver, and reflect back," he says. "Like you painted a mirror with nail polish." Brilliant, but brittle.

"Acetate will crack like glass. The harder the plastic the nicer the sequin's going to be."

When war was over, Mr. Lieberman went to work for his father. "I knew sequins," he says. "I wanted to find some new products."

Mr. Lieberman started producing costumes for Broadway shows. It didn't pan out. "If the show was a success, you got paid," he says. "If the show was a failure, you didn't get paid."

Algy made costumes for Shriners. "We made sequin headdresses, jackets, pants," he says. Shriners wear fezes. "They were coming in and spending thou –" He stops himself. He doesn't want to snitch on Shriners.

Mr. Lieberman worked on *The Jackie Gleason Show*. He made costumes for Gleason's costars, the June Taylor Dancers. "There were twelve or sixteen dancers," he says, "and we had to produce a set of costumes for them each week."

"Here it is Friday," Mr. Lieberman says, "and the show is Saturday night, and Jackie Gleason came up to the establishment. 'How do you expect the girls to dance in these?" he says. "They'll all break their necks, they're going to catch their heels!' I went and got him a big pair of shears," Mr. Lieberman continues. "All the girls stood there and he cut twelve inches off of those skirts." Mr. Lieberman laughs. He's 79 years old. "I'm having a blast remembering."

"Purdue University came out with their Golden Girl," Mr. Lieberman says. In 1954. The Golden Girl was a baton-twirler featured at football games.

"She wore the first all-over sequin uniform." Made by Algy. The company had a new name. Algy Dance Costume Company. "Band directors from all over the country started asking, 'Where did that costume come from?'"

Majorettes and marching bands became major markets. "Some of our products were terribly abused," he says. "They [customers] will go to the parade, and sit on the ground, or sit on a hard wooden bleacher bench. They can get them extremely dirty."

Plastic sequins were hardier than gelatin sequins. Still, they could melt in sun. And tarnish in rain. "We had to get around that eventually," he says. "It took many, many years. We experimented with different methods. What we came up with was a sandwich."

Mylar's the bread in the sandwich. Dupont developed Mylar during the war. To replace nylon in women's hose. "It's the plastic sequin with a piece of very thin, clear mylar around it," Mr. Lieberman says. "The colouring is actually inside. Protected." It'll survive a washing machine. Set on Gentle. And Cold. "I warn mothers, 'Don't put it in a dryer,'" he says. "Or we'll have very disappointed kids."

In 1970, Mr. Lieberman sold the sequin factory. He moved Algy to Florida. It became a catalogue company. "We narrowed our scope," he says. "The costume world is so vast. We concentrated on kiddie recital costumes. The other area where we concentrated was in the marching bands for high schools and colleges."

"Drum corps is very big in Canada," Susan Lieberman-Gordon tells me. Mr. Lieberman's daughter. She and her sister Laurie Godbout run Algy. She's joined the conversation. "You have two very competitive drum corps up there," she says. "And we have dance school clients in Canada, but no high school squads."

"Weather's our biggest enemy in Canada," Mr. Lieberman says. He retired in 1999. He still comes around the office. "I get no greater joy than seeing these kids come pick up their costumes," he says. "The minute a little girl puts on her fairy costume, she's a fairy. I get the best photos and letters."

Sequins aren't made with silver anymore. "Silver tarnished," he says. "As the air got in around the edges. Like your mirror turns black around the edges. Also, the cost of silver was getting prohibitive." New sequins come coated in aluminum. "The truth of the matter is that most sequins today aren't as brilliant."

"Today the sequins are made out of vinyl plastic," he says. "It's easier to work with. It's not brittle. The plating adheres to it better because it's a softer surface."

"Unfortunately, it will curl up as it gets older," he says. "Vinyl has a memory."

2003

THE BOTTOM OF THE POOL

"My favorite Hollywood suicide of all," Kenneth Anger said, "was Gwili Andre's." In the 1970s, in an interview with Roger Ebert, Anger listed all the filmland suicides he loved: besides Andre, there was Peg Entwistle and Lupe Velez. Why didn't he list Vera West?

Dracula. Frankenstein. The Mummy. The Wolf Man. The Invisible Man.

The great monster movies of Hollywood's golden age. They were all made by Universal. They were all worked on by Vera West, Universal's head costume designer.

Vera West dressed the principal actresses in monster movies. The principal actresses played victims for the most part—a mad scientist's fiancée, a mummy's long-lost love, a werewolf's crush— but sometimes they played villains. There were the three vampire wives in *Dracula*; there was Dracula's Daughter; there was the Bride of Frankenstein.

Haute horror—this is what West's remembered for. This and her death: "This is the only way. I am tired of being blackmailed." A suicide note. Vera West wrote it. Police found her floating in the pool behind her home on June 29, 1947.

There was a second suicide note. Scrawled in pencil on a torn greeting card: "The fortune teller told me there was only one way to duck the blackmail I've paid for twenty-three years… death."

"NOTED WOMAN SUICIDES DUE TO BLACKMAIL," stated the *San Jose Evening News*; "VERA WEST DEAD; WAS FILM STYLIST," stated an article from the Associated Press; "DESIGNER ENDS LIFE IN HOLLYWOOD," stated an article from United Press.

The story played in national papers for a spell. *The New York Times* reported that it would investigate the claims of blackmail. *The New York Times* never reported on it again.

There was never a probe, never a conviction, never a name named.

Was she being blackmailed? Was there a fortune teller? Who knows?

Vera West was born in New York City on June 28, 1900. She attended the Philadelphia Institute of Design, studying dressmaking with Lucile, Lady Duff-Gordon, a couturière with clienteles in London, Paris, and New York.

After graduation, West designed dresses for a salon on Fifth Avenue in New York City. She worked at the salon for four years. Then she committed a crime. She had an illicit affair. She had a child.

Something.

If her suicide note is to be believed, she became embroiled in some sordid, secret scenario in New York City that would haunt her for the rest of her life. Then: she fled to Hollywood.

The Man Who Laughed (1928) was the first picture for which West received credit onscreen. It starred Conrad Veidt as a man whose face had been surgically sculpted into a sinister smile.

Vera West had by this time become Universal's head of costume design, taking the place of Lucia Coulter. Sometimes her name didn't appear in credits. Sometimes she is listed as costumer. Sometimes it says, Gowns by Vera West; sometimes, Frocks by Vera West. In 1934, *Silver Screen* magazine referred to West as Wardrobe Supervisor. In 1938, an ad in *Silver Screen* called West a Costume Creator.

What did she create? How did she dress the actresses who appeared in monster movies?

For day, she favoured smart suits in tweed or wool, fringed with furbelows. The Carpathians could be cold. For evening, evening gowns in the style of Schiaparelli and Chanel. Almost all of West's women wound up wearing something white at night. A negligée. Or a wedding dress.

Vera West drowned herself in a nightie.

In 1931, Bela Lugosi played Dracula in Tod Browning's *Dracula*. Dracula desires Mina Seward, played by Helen

Chandler. West swathed her in white satin. When Universal shot a Spanish-language version of *Dracula* on the same stage sets, West sexed up the wardrobe. Décolletage deepened. Watch Lupita Tovar's character as she frolics with her boyfriend. Visible beneath her negligée—nipple.

In 1931's *Frankenstein*, Dr. Henry Frankenstein stitches together a monster from dead body parts. The monster—Boris Karloff with bolts in his skull—frightens Frankenstein's fiancée, whose wardrobe seems to consist of nothing but white lace gowns. Her wedding dress is beaded, embroidered, the train twenty feet long and covered with fancywork flowers. It wasn't West's most famous wedding dress. Elsa Lanchester played the monster's betrothed in *The Bride of Frankenstein* of 1935. Her ensemble: a gown cut from white surgical sheets, opera gloves made of bandages.

It's difficult to know if West designed the Bride's outfit by herself, or if she had help from James Whale, the film's director. As horror historian David J. Skal has said, "[S]adly, not a single costume sketch from any of the classic horror films seems to have survived."

Universal cranked out monster movies in the decades that West worked for it. She costumed actresses in *The Invisible Man*. And in *The Invisible Man Returns*. And *The Invisible Man's Revenge*. After *The Mummy*, she made *The Mummy's Hand*, *The Mummy's Curse*, *The Mummy's Ghost*, and *The Mummy's Tomb*.

Frankenstein's monster returned to the screen as *The Ghost of Frankenstein*.

The Wolf Man? He dies in the original movie. He rises from the grave in *Frankenstein Meets the Wolf Man*. He's miserable. He begs Dr. Frankenstein's daughter to cure him. Or kill him. In *House of Dracula*, he takes matters into his own hands. About to change into a wolf, he leaps into the ocean, desperate to drown.

Vera West, it seems, was as tired of costuming the Wolf Man as he was of turning into a wolf. In early 1947, she resigned her role at Universal.

Mere months later she murdered herself.

Kenneth Anger, connoisseur of suicides, hasn't written about Vera West's life or death; he is, however, a fan of her work. *Cobra Woman*, he says, is his favourite film.

Cobra Woman (1944) tells the tale of Tollea, an exile from Cobra Island, and her twin sister, Naja, who rules the island as the hateful high priestess.

The sister roles are played by a single actress, Maria Montez, called the Queen of Technicolor for the escapist tropical pictures she made during World War Two.

The costumes? They were Vera West's. The highlight is the dress worn by Naja during the Cobra Dance of Death. It's sewn to seem like a cobra skin, but in colours cobras aren't. It's pistachio and avocado. Scales are sequins.

Kenneth Anger played hooky from school to see the film when it was released. He said it was "perfect."

Jack Smith saw the film in 1951 while he was working as an usher at a movie palace in Chicago. He came to call Montez the "Holy One," and the "Miraculous One," and later he said of her: "The Miraculous One was raging and flaming. Those are the standards for art."

Flaming Creatures and *Normal Love* (1963), Smith's features, were homages to Montez and the technicolor pictures she made for Universal—*Ali Baba & the Forty Thieves*, *Arabian Nights*, and *Cobra Woman*. They were also, in a way, homages to era West, who created Montez's technicolor clothes: Smith's monsters —his vampires and mermaids and mummies and werewolves—are wearing Wests they compose from whatever shimmery second-hand crap they can.

"These were light films," Jack Smith said of Montez's movies. "[I]f we believed that films are visual it would be possible to believe these as rather pure cinema—weak technique, true, but rich imagery … The primitive allure of movies is a thing of light and shadows."

Kenneth Anger, who considers his camera a wand, sees his own films as invocations of spells that summoned Lucifer, the bearer of light.

"I'm an artist working in Light, and that's my whole interest, really," said Anger. "Lucifer is the Light God, not the devil, that's a Christian slander. The devil is always other people's gods."

In the book *Light Moving in Time*, film theorist William Wees views Anger's visions through a prism provided by Aldous Huxley; and, specifically, through what Huxley termed "preternatural light." Preternatural light, writes Wees, *pace* Huxley, is provided by those materials in our world "that are most luminescent, most intensely glowing with color, and therefore most like the object seen by the visionary."

Gemstones, pearls, gold and silver, crystal and glass— preternatural light pours from these things, said Huxley. Anger felt that films possessed the same light: films were for him illuminated from within. It wasn't enough to see them; as Anger said in an interview, "[I] wanted to create a feeling of being carried into a world of wonder… in other words, it expands, it becomes completely subjective—like when people take communion."

Film, Anger is saying, is eucharist; it is consumed.

The gown that Vera West made for *Cobra Woman* was magic. It was film itself, a visionary light. It constituted a Satanic communion: audiences drank in her sequins, and were sanctified.

What's more preternatural than a pool sparkling under the Hollywood stars? West's suicide was itself a Satanic communion—it's true that her pool swallowed her; it's true, too, that she swallowed her pool.

James Whale drowned himself in his pool in 1957. "Do not grieve for me," his suicide note said, "the future is just old age and illness and pain." Maria Montez drowned in a bathtub in Paris in 1951. Fans have speculated forever that it was suicide. A friend of Maria's claims that there was a suicide note. In it, Maria said that she did not want to get old.

She hasn't.

Afterword to *The Bottom of the Pool*

"My grandmother knew Busby Berkeley, and he was cruel," Kenneth Anger told *The Guardian*. "In *Footlight Parade*, he had girls dive into the shallow water and their knees were scraped bloody. The water was stained pink by the time he was finished."

Preternatural light glitters all through Kenneth Anger's films—in the puce sequins in *Puce Moment*; in the water in *Eaux d'Artifice*, in which the Water Witch—costumed as Marie Antoinette—walks through fountains and then metamorphoses into sprays.

The colour pink itself has preternatural power in Anger. Think of *Kustom Kar Kommandoes*, in which a beefcake boy buffs a car with a fluffy duster against a pink backdrop. The colour pink itself is a preternatural light beloved by avant-garde gay filmmakers of the past. Think of Jack Smith—think of the pink beads, the pink glitter. *Normal Love*, the colour follow-up to Flaming Creatures, was at different times titled *The Pink and Green Film*, *The Pink and Green Horrors*, *The Rose and Green Horrors*, *The Moonpool Film*. Think of James Bidgood—*Pink Narcissus*. Think of John Waters—*Pink Flamingos*. Think of Andy Warhol—well, think of his screen prints of Marilyn on hot pink, and his cows.

Think pink. There is the matter, too, of decay and fading in film. In 1950, Kodak introduced Eastmancolor—it used a single strip of film for shooting, where Technicolor required three separate rolls to be shot in order to strike a print. The thing is, Kodachrome and Technicolor didn't fade. By the early 1970s, however, it was clear that the same was not true for Eastmancolor. The films were fading even when stored in metal or plastic cans. This is how it went—the yellow dye layer died, and then the cyan dye layer died, leaving magenta.

The result: gay magic—Hollywood films turning as pink as faggy films.

"What was once a color film is now a jarring mixture of faded dyes in a spectrum that runs from dull, muddy pink to deep, garish purple. The sunny windswept fields of *Oklahoma!* have turned an eerie strident pink. Marilyn Monroe looks jaundiced." This from *Film Comment* in 1979.

Jack Tillmany of the Gateway Cinema in SF said this in 1980: "We are presently presenting the only 35mm print 'in service' of the 1963 Academy Award winner, *Tom Jones*, 'Color by Deluxe.' The vivid greens that were so vital to the marvelous photography of this film that remain in the memory of those of us who saw it in 1963 are now just that: a memory. The whole damn thing has turned fire-engine red. Tom Jones is now romping across a red countryside under pink skies. Thank you, Eastman Kodak."

There are three things I want to say about this:

1) The fading color, the decaying dyes, is turning the films gay. What's fascinating is that gay filmmakers and their pink

palettes foresaw this filmic decay and made it an aesthetic.

2) The films are turning gay because they were always gay—
this decadence is a divine sign reminding us that film, as
Anger always says, is Satanic—its "natural" light, concocted by
Hollywood, is being burned off by the preternatural.

3) The sun isn't natural, it's preternatural—the sun, the
sequin to end all sequins, the gem to end all gems, is Satanic,
and the visionaries who see this are fags. It's like that line in
Bob Dylan's "Tombstone Blues": "The sun's not pink, it's
faggy."

2018

THE DEVIL-DOLLS

Viktor & Rolf are dolls.

Viktor Horsting and Rolf Snoeren, the Dutch fashion designers known for conceptually-inflected clothing and fragrances, are living dolls: smiling, solicitous, and of surprisingly similar stature—it's as if they were made in the same mold.

The duo was in Toronto recently to promote their brand and to talk about—what else?—dolls. Since 2008, they've been designing porcelain dolls and dressing them in small-scale versions of some of the same outfits they display in their Paris *defilés*. Starting June 9, Toronto's Luminato Festival is presenting these dolls to the public at the Royal Ontario Museum; though Viktor & Rolf won't be attending the festival, they'll be there in spirit—or rather, in porcelain, in the form of the figurines they outfit.

"It will be like a runway," Viktor says of *Dolls by Viktor & Rolf*, "a specially-designed runway, and the dolls will model on it."

The show will constitute a sort of survey of Viktor & Rolf's twenty years in fashion. The dolls will be wearing the most memorable designs from the duo's collections; the dolls themselves will depict the actual models who first wore the designs. An Erin O'Connor doll, for instance, in a dress sewn from fabric flowers from 2003, or a Karolina Kurkova doll in gown of gold and pink ribbons from 2005.

The showstopper is sure to be the Maggie Rizer doll. At Viktor and Rolf's Autumn/Winter 1999 show, Viktor and Rolf dressed Rizer in ten different layers, from slip to spangly gown to brocaded coat; at the end, she was immobile, unable to move her limbs—mannequin as mannequin. The collection, which was titled "Russian Doll," brought the designers international attention and demonstrated the depth of their affection for dolls and the effects that they can conjure: the inanimate made animate, the miniature made large, the body doubled. The designers themselves play with these ideas: they dress, speak and act alike. Though they aren't twins (or lovers, by the by), they seem to have fun with the confusion: which one is Viktor and which is Rolf?

"There are a few doubles," Rolf says of his doll collection, "but for the most part the dolls are unique. It takes so much time and work to produce each one—there's no way we could do multiples."

The dolls are produced at a doll factory in Belgium. They stand seventy centimeters or so. Facial features are sculpted, then paint is applied to capture the makeup the models wore. The heads are then glazed five times, in order to set the colours. A hairdresser works on the wigs, which are woven from human hair. Seamstresses at the Viktor & Rolf studio in Amsterdam sew the dolls' wardrobe.

"The same women who work on the couture," Rolf says, "are working on the dolls."

"The dolls are our archive," Viktor says. "We don't own all of our old creations. In some cases, museums have them; in some cases, the only copies are on the dolls."

The dolls are stored at a facility in Amsterdam. Each figure has its own wood box. "Its own coffin," Viktor laughs. He continues: "It will be like in *Dracula*, all the coffins crossing the ocean to come to Canada." It's a creepy image, and the pair delight in it it. Dolls can be beautiful, yes, but they can also be disturbing, a fact that the designers trade on.

"We love things that are surreal," Rolf says. Avid art collectors, the duo is drawn to the work of David Altmejd, the Canadian sculptor who filled the Canadian pavilion at the 2007 Venice Biennial with werewolves, men with bird heads, and giants made of mirror fragments and crystalline rocks. "This is very much our style," Rolf says, flipping through a book by the Canadian artist Shary Boyle, who is representing the country at this year's Biennial. Boyle is well-known for her porcelain dolls, which are delicate depictions of grotesqueries—in a sculpture from 2005, a lady holds her own head in her hands. It's as if the Brothers Grimm supervised a shift at Royal Doulton.

The designers bring to mind the British artists Gilbert and George, who work as a pair, present their art as a pair, and even move with a puppet-like precision. Viktor and Rolf cite another inspiration: the Canadian collective General Idea. "General Idea were doing things that we like to do with image and with critiquing fashion." The men in General Idea—Felix Partz, Jorge Zontal and A.A. Bronson—spoke as a single entity, and once styled themselves as cherubic babies: in an image from 1985, they appear in bed as triplets, as rosy-cheeked as Kewpies. They played with their personae like they were playing with toys. It's a distancing effect that Viktor and Rolf wield well—it lends them an otherworldliness, an opaqueness, an artiness.

"They have a strange presence," Rolf says, referring to his dolls, though he could be referring to himself and his partner. He smiles. "It's almost as if they have souls."

2013

THE HAUNTED DOLLS' HOUSE

"The Haunted Dolls' House" was written by M.R. James in the 1920s[1]. James, it's said, was the father of the English ghost story; if his wasn't the first ghost story about a haunted dollhouse, it was the first to be well-known.[2] And influential: its spirit can be seen in a slew of incarnations, literary and otherwise—from the Doll's House Illusion, a staple of stage magicians, to Ideal's Haunted House, a board game.

Richard Hawkins is an American artist who recently had a retrospective at the Art Institute of Chicago. Hawkins works in myriad media. *Richard Hawkins: Third Mind*, the retrospective in Chicago, included samples from many of them: paintings, collages, sculptures, found objects he'd altered.

Dollhouses—Hawkins works with them, too. *Third Mind* featured a pair of his haunted dollhouse sculptures, both from 2010: *The Last House* and *Dilapidarian Tower*. He made them the way he made earlier dollhouse pieces: he doctored store-bought dollhouses—rearranging and reassembling them, then redecorating them to look eerie and decrepit. They're Frankensteinian monsters: part art, part toys, part puzzles, part Halloween ornaments. They're lit from inside; they're part lamps.

The Last House is a ramshackle Victorian made up of multiple ramshackle Victorians. It rises up and out, growing larger as it goes: a metastasizing mansion, a haunted house turning into a haunted slum. *Dilapidarian Tower* is eight storeys tall, a doll tower constructed from dollhouse salvage. It's streamlined, or it could be, if there weren't a porch tacked on here, a balcony there. On a couple porches, laundry hangs from laundry lines. Ghosts do laundry? Ghosts wear clothes? Q: What did the ghost in the Comme des Garçons store say? A: I'd be caught dead in that.[3]

If there's a Jamesian history of haunted doll houses, there's a hidden history, too: a Hawkinsian history in which dollhouses are haunted not by dolls, but by ideas.

In "The Haunted Dolls' House," James established an enduring blueprint for haunted dollhouses.

The dollhouse shows no signs of being haunted: the façade is flawless; the furnishings—chairs, beds, buffets and tables—are faithful reproductions of those found in historic homes.

In the decades that followed, it came to be a cliché of haunted dollhouse stories, from *The Dollhouse Mystery* by Carolyn Keene to *The Dollhouse Murders* by Betty Ren Wright: exemplary exteriors and immaculate interiors disturbed by spooky doings.

In "The Haunted Dolls' House," it's not the house that's haunted; it's the dolls.

The Mom and Dad dolls murder the grandfather doll for money; later, a demon that looks like a frog with a fringe of gray hair on his head murders Mom and Dad's son and daughter.

Since James's story, it's been the same: the same in *Hell* by Kathryn Davis as in *The Haunted Mansion Mystery*, a Barbie book: in an ornate dollhouse, appointed with period accoutrements, dolls act out the mad, murderous passions that humans attempt to tamp down.

In 1945, the writer Flora Gill Jacobs came across a dollhouse in the barn of a New Jersey antique dealer.

"It was cobwebbed and dirty," she later wrote in *A World of Doll Houses*, "with a number of broken windows. Until it was repaired, it was always thought of as 'the haunted house.'"

It was the first dollhouse she ever bought. Then she bought another. And another. She became a dollhouse collector and scholar: *A World of Doll Houses*, which was published in 1953, was the first survey of the subject. She wrote *The Doll House Mystery*, a Jamesian tale that unfolds in her New Jersey dollhouse. She went on to found the Washington Doll House and Toy Museum, the first museum of its kind in the United States. There she showcased her "haunted house," which was no longer haunted: she'd polished it up and appointed it with the proper Victoriana.

What makes a dollhouse look haunted?

For Flora Gill Jacobs, it was dereliction and disrepair.

Spooks? Spectres? Superfluous. To Jacobs, hauntedness was communicated not through devilry, but décor.

It's too bad that Jacobs repaired her New Jersey house: in its dirty condition, it represented a break from the Jamesian dollhouse and a harbinger of Richard Hawkins's works.

Hawkins's dollhouses aren't being disturbed, or about to be disturbed; they are disturbed. What disturbed them seems secondary to the damage it did. Hawkins seems to be saying: Shouldn't a haunted doll house look haunted? There are no dolls in Richard Hawkins's dollhouses; there are few if any furnishings. Hawkins is asking: Must a dollhouse be haunted by dolls? Must a dollhouse be haunted by something— anything—or might it simply be haunted: haunted by hauntedness?

A dollhouse on a table on a stage.

A magician opens it up: it's empty.

After closing it, he says abracadabra and—*voilà!*—conjures a doll: actually an assistant, a woman, always a woman. The dollhouse flies open, the roof flies off and she's atop the table, dollhouse around her feet.

How did he do that? The secret's simple: a false back in the dollhouse, a false top in the table, an assistant able to contort herself until it's time to stand up.

The Doll's House Illusion was created by the English comedian and magician Fred Culpitt, and dates to 1927, a mere two years after M.R. James published "The Haunted Dolls' House."[4]

By World War II, the illusion was being copied by acts in every country. Suppliers sold plans for a slight variation: an Oriental Doll House Illusion. "Magic!," an exhibit of magic history at the Houston Museum of Natural Science in 2009, showcased such a house: a standard Doll's House Illusion painted like a pagoda, with winged eaves slapped onto the structure.

"The Madhouse of Mystery"—Bill Neff, an American magician, toured a show with this name in the years after World War II.

It was a spook show. It played movie palaces. Before a monster movie screened, Neff would run through a series of sinister-seeming illusions—the Spirit Cabinet, the Cremation Illusion, the Frame of Life and Death illusion—against a frightening backdrop: a forest full of buzzards and bats.

The Doll's House Illusion was part of his presentation. In this incarnation it had a sinister spin: his house was black, with glow-in-the-dark door and window frames. A doll didn't rise from it; a ghost did, a woman in a white sheet and hood.

The show ended with a blackout: theatre lights died, and spooks and skeletons suspended from strings swept out over the crowd.

Then the movie started.

The Doll's House Illusion belongs to both the Jamesian and the Hawkinsian traditions: it bridges them.

As in James's story, the dollhouse in Culpitt's illusion was a locus for magic. In "The Haunted Dolls' House," the magic's supernatural; in the Doll's House Illusion, it's a trick tricked out to seem supernatural.

A haunted dollhouse that looks haunted—the dollhouse that Bill Neff designed for his Madhouse of Mystery presaged Hawkins's sculptures by decades. Then again, so did the pagoda dollhouses that magic suppliers peddled. Hawkins's sculptures aren't only haunted by the idea of hauntedness; they're haunted by Orientalism, too. And sodomy:

Bordello on rue St. Lazare (2007) is an early dilapidated dollhouse. It depicts the boy brothel where Proust liked to play. On a wall: a portrait of Proust. The building's abandoned: no dolls. It's boarded-up, but badly—furnishings have been left behind, an Oriental rug, some Japanese vases, a

Chinese palace lantern with red tassels.

Stairwell Down, another dollhouse from 2007, is a dead ringer for the *Bordello*, save that it's not decorated in an Orientalist style. Instead of sitting on a tabletop, *Stairwell Down* is stuck to the table's underside, hanging upside-down like a stalactite, or snot. It seems to point straight down to China, or Istanbul, or Siam, or Shangri-La—and to the boys who sell themselves there.[5]

The Haunted House by Ideal is a board game from 1962. It's black; the box is decorated with bats. It's a dollhouse of sorts: a very shallow Victorian with visible rooms. In its day, it was the only board game that stood upright on a tabletop. Players spin an owl spinner, proceed through the rooms. In each room, a locked door. Stick a plastic key into a door and a message pops out: "Go back to Room B." Stick a key into another door: "Go to the start." Another key, another door: a ghost pops out. There's a prize concealed in the attic: a plastic ruby.

The Hootin' Hollow Haunted House by Marx was released at around the same time as the Haunted House. It's made of metal—tin that's been lithographed with broken windows and broken clapboard. What appear to be typewriter keys protrude from the side of it. Press a key: a ghost swoops across a window. Press a key: a vampire pops out of the chimney top.

Dollhouses are for girls. When a boy wants a dollhouse, he's faggy. When faggy boys grow up, they become fags.

In the 1960s, toy companies began selling dollhouses for boys. They weren't called dollhouses: they were games, or playsets. They didn't look like Barbie's Dream House: they were macabre, the more macabre the better. Dream House? Dread House. Built not for Barbie, but for Barbey d'Aurevilly. Boys were allowed to want them. The Haunted House game was cool. Mad Monster Castle by Mego was cool: Mad Monster action figures played there. Action figures sold separately. The castle was cardboard—pink cardboard.

The Weebles had a Haunted House. It wasn't so cool.

A lot of the art in *Third Mind* has a toylike taste. *disembodied zombie skeet pink* (1997) is a print of Skeet Ulrich— his detached bleeding head, anyway—floating on a pink field. It's from a series: there are disembodied Bens and Johns and Georges, too.

The zombie boys remind me of the dates in Mystery Date, a board game from 1965. In that game, girls tried to get a good date: the bowling date, or the skiing date, or the formal dance date; in Hawkins's hand, ghouls come calling, and they're cute. Black tassels of blood drip off them.

Shinjuku Labyrinth (2007) has a board game feel to it, too. It's a maze made of scale-model wood fence slats; in the maze's dead-ends are collaged characters, cute male pop stars and movie idols, clipped from the pages of Japanese and Chinese magazines.

Arrayed on a black tabletop, and assembled from artfully worn and falling-down wood, the labyrinth a scary affair: the boys cruising within it are uprights, like the spook pieces in Disney's Haunted Mansion board game. It radiates desperation, dark desire, and a playful sense of toy design: Fisher Price by Vincent Price.

But what does it mean when grown men have haunted dollhouses?

"The Haunted Dolls' House" was haunted by faggotry in the form of Mr. Dillet, an adult– without wife or children—who lived among the gems of his dollhouse collection. And what about the frog-faced ghoul with gray hair? Don't gays love to murder children?

With dollhouses as with lovers, some open in the front, and some open in the rear. Which way do Richard Hawkins's haunted dollhouses open? I don't know. Maybe they don't open; maybe they open in ways no dollhouse has ever done before. They're gay and more: transvestite, transgendered, between and beyond genders. Dollhouses in decadent drag. Desire haunts them; in turn, they expose and exaggerate the desire and its seemingly supernatural powers.

In dollhouses, boys are always toys.

2011

Footnotes to *The Haunted Dolls' House*

1. 'The Haunted Dolls' House' was first published in 1925. M.R. James died in 1936.

2. M.R. James was gay, though it's not known if he ever acted on it; he certainly never wrote about gay sex. He liked to grab his students and roll around with them; he called it "ragging." He was provost of King's College, Cambridge (1905–1918) and of Eton College (1918–1936).

3. *Third Mind* also features Hawkins's *House of the Mad Professor* (2008). It's a wooden black box with windows. Someone peeping into it sees a scale-model residence decorated with Chinoiserie, Japonisme, and classical statues. The residence is rigged with mirrors, so it's hard to tell what's real, what's a reflection, and how deep it actually is.

4. Fred Culpitt was a protégé of Chung Ling Soo's, the world-famous Chinese conjurer. Culpitt knew what the world didn't: that Soo wasn't Chinese. Soo's real name was William Robinson, and he was really a Scot living in Brooklyn. As Soo, Robinson wore a black wig with a black ponytail and a wardrobe picked up in New York's Chinatown. When performing with Soo, Culpitt would sometimes get himself up in comical Chinese garb and call himself Chow Fat; his assistant would call herself Char Ming. Culpitt also starred in the George Formby film *Keep Your Seats, Please* (1936). He played a conjurer named Marasking.

5. I own blueprints for building a Doll's House Illusion. They were published by the Abbott Magic Company of Colon, Ohio. In the 1950s, Abbott's operated a retail store in the Woods Building on Randolph St. in Chicago. The store was on the second floor, above the Woods Theater, a movie palace. The Woods' façade was done in the Venetian Renaissance style; the interior was a blend of Middle Eastern and Oriental styles. The building, theatre and all, was demolished in the 1990s. The Goodman Theatre Center now sits in the site. The Goodman is owned by the Art Institute of Chicago.

WHAT I KNOW ABOUT WOMEN
Publishing with Pas de Chance

Christmas is coming. Ian Phillips tends a table at the Small Press Book Fair in Toronto. He's the proprietor of Pas de Chance press. He's displaying his haunting, handmade books. Beside the books: a plate piled with snowballs.

"Sold any?" I say.

"No one knows what they are," he says.

Faux—an essay about the history of fake snow in Canada. I wrote it. Someone had to! Borax. Broken glass. Asbestos flakes. Flour. Since Confederation, Canadians have decorated Christmas trees with fake snow made from all manner of materials.

Pas de Chance published my essay as a book. Phillips designed it, printed it, bound it. The spine a simple stitch. He illustrated it: a snowman on skis takes a spill on the slopes. A snowman gets an x-ray. His lungs are snow. The book's small, enclosure card-size. He enclosed it in snowballs he sculpted.

He tried papier-mâché. Snowballs turned out too delicate. They warped. He tried plaster of Paris. He settled on sculpting clay. Hobby stores sell it. It hardens in a hurry. Moulds came from a cosmetics company. Moulds usually used to make bath bombs. He painted his snowballs white, sprayed them with aerosol snow. Silvered them with sparkles.

"Maybe we should put a sign up," I say. "'Snowballs Are Books.'"

"Maybe," he says, "we should have a demonstration model."

What is the history of fake snowballs in Canada? In a novelty catalogue from the 1940s, Phillips came across snowball-shaped Christmas crackers. They were paper, packed with the gimcrackery that all crackers contain: tissue paper party hats, prizes, riddles or verses.

"You can't buy them anymore," says Phillips, who based the look of *Faux* on these bygone snowball crackers. Eaton's sold them. Simpson's. A box cost a dollar. People put them on plates, making centrepieces. People hung them on trees. Stores sold blue snowballs.

"I called a Christmas cracker company. They used to use round paper shells for the balls. They didn't have any more." Shells would have saved him time. It takes him an hour to finish a snowball. He stuffs it with my book, and with fake snow made from mica flakes. Seals it shut.

"It's a little larger than a cracker," he says, picking up a copy of *Faux*. "A little heavier." It's a little like a lot of things. A Cracker Jack box with a prize inside. A plastic bubble in a gumball machine. A snow globe. An iced-over snow globe. A wintry world we can't see. How it's like a cracker: to get to the goodies, the snowball must be broken. "That's the fun of it. I love the sound it makes."

He drops it. He laughs.

"Quality works of art at fair prices." That's how Phillips
described his work in a Pas de Chance mail-order catalogue
from 2000. "You will find the same high quality and
reasonable prices we have always maintained since the
establishment of our press in 1985."

For decades, Phillips has run Pas de Chance from the house
he shares with his boyfriend, Grant Heaps, in downtown
Toronto. He has a degree in graphic design. Freelance book
and advertising design pays his bills. Newpapers such as *The
New York Times* and *Xtra!* run his illustrations. In 2002,
Princeton Architectural Press put out *LOST*, a book of lost pet
posters culled from his personal collection. *LOST* sold tens of
thousands of copies. Paycheques he pours into Pas de Chance.
Profit's never been the point. He pays out of pocket to produce
his books. They rarely recoup. No matter—he's free to do as he
pleases.

What does it please him to do? Books of poetry, prose,
photography, found art. Common characteristics: they all look
unlike. They all look unlike any other book ever published.
They're scarce, sold only through an online store, and at fairs.
The mail-order catalogues are collectibles. Like *Faux*, Pas de
Chance books can require a reader's interaction, above and
beyond the act of reading. Like *Faux*, they can be ephemeral.
Enjoying them might mean destroying them. Phillips wants it

this way. He wants to know: as a reader alters a Pas de Chance book, is the book also altering the reader?

Faux confuses customers.

"There's a book inside?" a lady says, listening to a snowball.

"I have to break it?" a man asks. "I'm not buying it to break it!"

So buy something else. Pas de Chance's table brims with books. Among them: *Artist & Models*, erotic cartoons by Maurice Vellekoop. *Angels of Demise*, stories about nurses convicted of killing patients. *Sleeping Beauties*, a fanzine devoted to *Grey Gardens*, David and Albert Maysles's movie about Edith and Little Edie Bouvier.

The designs are dead on. *Artist & Models* is modelled on men's pornographic magazines of the 1970s. *Angels of Demise* is printed on heat-sensitive paper: it changes colours in a reader's hands, from gangrenous green to cirrhotic yellow. *Sleeping Beauties* comes with a selection of sheet music, songs Little Edie sings in the film.

"The content decides the design," Phillips says. "I'm inspired by novelty. I try and take something from a book—a scene, or a tone, or an object. I try to make it real. I do it with whatever means might work."

Drinking Songs is a collection of poetry by Elissa Joy, a perennial Pas de Chance collaborator. Decorating the cover: a crushed cocktail umbrella. The book includes a sheet of stick-on tattoos shaped like martini olives. "The umbrellas are so pretty," he says. "People play with them at bars, put them in their hair. They last as long as the fun. The tattoos will last longer."

The cover of Joy's *Quinceañera* has a cut-out hole. Bulging through it: an eyeball. A toy. Are you reading the book, or it reading you?

"*Quinceañera* has poems about Saint Lucy of Syracuse," he says. "She had her eyes gouged out. She carried them around. She could still see."

"In your book, in *Faux*," he says, "all the kinds of snow are so makeshift. Pinning popcorn to trees. Asbestos flakes. I wanted the book to be like that. To be makeshift. Temporary. Like what it describes.

"I put a copy of *Faux* in a friend's mailbox," he says. "She didn't know what it was. She threw it in a snow bank." He gave a copy to a female friend who hung it on her Christmas tree. Her husband thought it tacky. He threw it out without cracking it. Phillips smiles. "That seems perfect."

Faux marks my third collaboration with Pas de Chance. In 1998, we published *Halloween Suite*, a cycle of short stories; in 2002, *Western Suit*, a novella. *Halloween Suite* looks like the book a character in *Halloween Suite* is peddling. *Western Suit* resembles a sewing pattern envelope. It comes with a custom-made pattern. The novella's about a country star, his wife, and a vampire tailor.

"I want to make the books come to life," he says. "But I want to make life part of the books, too. *Faux*'s about how disposable and dangerous holidays can be. When a reader breaks a snowball, he adds to the waste. When he cuts a pattern, or puts on tattoos, or sings a song—he's part of the plot." The book is his world, or the world is his book. "He's doing what the characters do. He becomes a character."

I first met Phillips in 1997. A mutual friend made the introductions at the Old Paper Show, a sale of paper ephemera that takes place twice a year in Toronto.

I was buying Bogie Books. The Dennison Paper Manufacturing Co. of Massachusetts put them out in the 1920s and 1930s. Manuals for planning posh Halloween parties. How to make skeletons and witches from crepe? How to make nut cups from crepe? How to turn a basement into a pirate's cave with crepe? Bogie Books told all.

Dennison manufactured crepe paper.

"It was meant to look old," Phillips says.

He's remembering how we made *Halloween Suite*. In the stories, a character named "The Emcee" visits Peterborough, Ontario. My hometown. It's the Depression. He claims to be an expert in Halloween. He peddles his book, *Halloween Carnival*

Time! He decorates the city, arranging activities for the citizens. While the population parties, he murders a little boy.

Phillips imagined what *Halloween Carnival Time!* would've looked like. He illustrated it with images from Bogie Books. Black cats. Black bats. Screaming skulls in black top hats. He printed it in orange and black ink on off-colour paper. The cheapest paper the printer had. It looked yellow. Past its prime. Peaked. For dingbats, he drew bats.

"I went a little crazy on the covers." Phillips flocked them. "I found green flocking at a hardware store in Toronto. I bought a bag so I could get the name of the supplier. Then I ordered orange flocking from the States."

Flocking feels like felt. After it's applied. In the bag, it's polyester powder. He coated book boards in glue, then sprayed it on with a flocking gun. Flocking flew. "Someone told me that it was dangerous to breathe it in," he says. "I didn't feel anything."

From Texas came a cattle brand. Custom-made. He designed the branding mark: a jolly jack-o'-lantern. "I could've gotten one that heated on a gas stove, but that seemed to be a bother." He opted for electrical. He heated it, then branded the covers. It burned the flocking. The smoke was pure poison. "I ended up doing them outside in the wind," he says.

Halloween Suite made its debut at Canzine, a festival of zines and small presses, in 1998. "I think we charged twenty dollars," Phillips says. "It didn't cover the cost of the book. I wanted kids to afford it." He bagged them in Halloween grab bags, as if they were candy corn or kisses.

"Everyone liked the card." The book contained a paper pocket, like in old library books. He stamped it: PETERBOROUGH PUBLIC LIBRARY. And: DISCARDED. In the pocket: a withdrawal card. According to the card, the book had been checked out every Halloween night from 1935 to 1957.

"So many people asked me if it was really an old library book," he says. The card and the discarded stamp endowed *Halloween Suite* with a history. An untraceable, unknowable history. According to the stamp, the book had been disposed off. And had returned. A ghost. Book as bogie man.

"I used to see books advertised in the back of comic books," he says. Snake books—open them and snakes jump out. Exploding books—open them a cap detonates. Gag books like *I Cover the Waterfront*—open it and find a miniature diaper pinned to the pages. *What I Know About Women*—a book that's blank on the inside. Pranks. Books as one-liners. "I saw a copy of *Halloween Suite* for resale online," he says. "It said 'Ex-library.'" Halloween book as Halloween stunt. "It made me happy."

Halloween night, 2002. Skeletons, witches, werewolves—costumed people parade up and down Church St. in Toronto.

Then they stop, stare. Striding down the sidewalk—a pair of jeans. The jeans are six feet high and nearly as wide. The right leg takes a step. The left leg takes a step. The pants try to hail a taxi. Taxis tear by. A policeman pulls over a taxi, and helps the pants into the back seat.

"I was in the right leg," Grant Heaps says. "Ian was in the left. One of us would shuffle ahead, then say, 'Stop,' and then the other one would move ahead. Heaps giggles. "It was wild. People were poking us. People were yelling at us. We could see them through mesh I'd sewn at eye level. They couldn't see us."

For years, Heaps has made Halloween costumes for himself and Phillips. In 2003, they were sock monkeys. "I tore up two hundred pairs of wool socks to make those suits," he says. In 2005, they were sea monkeys, the pets that used to be sold in comic books. Sea monkeys are brine shrimp, also known as fairy shrimp. Heaps sewed the suits from stretch velvet.

Heaps is an assistant to the Chief Costumer of the National Ballet of Canada. After work, he creates exquisite and complicated quilts from cast-off fabrics: old silk neckties, for example. He is also a hidden force of Pas de Chance. He and Phillips have been boyfriends for almost twenty years. Heaps advises, consults, critiques. He also sews: at work, tutus; at home, spines. He has a Singer machine set up in Phillips's studio.

"*Western Suit* couldn't have been made without him," Phillips says.

Western Suit recounts the rise and fall of Hank, a country-and-western singer. In an early scene, Hank tries on a new suit. His wife sewed it. From a pattern: Western Suit by the Cowpoke Pattern Co.

Western Suit is fiction. There were no such people. I made it up. Phillips made it real. When he decided to publish my novella, he decided that it would take the form of Hank's wife's pattern.

He and Heaps bought western shirt patterns on eBay. Vintage 1940s. Heaps cut them up, then combined them into something new. Shortening a sleeve, widening a collar, substituting snaps for buttons. Patterns come in paper sleeves. Phillips designed his own sleeve. He added an illustration. He added a credit: Cowpoke Pattern Co.

Phillips sent his sleeve to a printer in Toronto. He sent Heaps's pattern to McCall's, one of the largest pattern manufacturers in the United States. McCall's ran off copies on professional pattern paper, on pattern-making machines. Two thousand copies—McCall's minimum order. They folded them, then shipped them back. Bundles bound in wire.

There was only one thing missing from my book: a book.

Phillips illustrated and printed my novella. Heaps sewed signatures. He cut covers from flocked paper that felt like suedine. A clothing company custom-made woven cloth labels: *WS*, they said, brown letters on a yellow base. Heaps whip-stitched a label to the front of each cover. Into every sleeve, he and Phillips stuffed a pattern, pattern instructions, and a copy of the book. It took hours.

Western Suit is for sale at the Small Press Book Fair. Men, Phillips finds, haven't a clue what it is. Women peg it as a sewing pattern—a memory from Home Economics class in high school?

"I know a couple people who used the pattern," he says. Heaps made himself a shirt with the flocked paper that covered the book. "Some readers unfolded the pattern and couldn't refold it.

"Some people bought two *Western Suits*, one to use, one to save. I got an email from a lady in Kentucky, or Tennessee. She ordered *Western Suit.* She said she'd been looking for a pattern with that particular collar. She said she didn't want the book. She said the book sounded crazy.

"A pattern's a sort of book, I don't know if it has a name." Coupon books. Colouring books. Department store catalogues. Books of ride tickets from Walt Disney World. "They're not supposed to last." Built-in obsolescence. "There's something beautiful about that."

Ants in armor, ants armed with swords—an army of ants assembles under a toadstool. A scout ant stares into the distance. An ant in epaulettes— a commandant?—holds a telescope in his legs.

"I don't know who they're fighting," Ian Phillips says. "Anteaters?"

I'm looking at *Funeral*, Pas de Chance's latest production.

"The man up the street died," he says. "His house was for sale. I think he was a graphic designer. I found a film strip. A Sunday school cartoon. I don't know if he worked on it. Maybe he taught Sunday school. I took it. Cut it up. I transferred frames onto iron-on transfer paper."

A slug reclines in a cave, puffing on a pipe. A stormy sea tosses mice from a rowboat. A honeybee feeds her hungry children from stone honey pots. Animals pop up throughout *Funeral*. He ironed transfers to white pages, then pressed white pages between black pages. Black carbon paper. I flip through the book again, and again. My hands heat it. My hands apply pressure. Carbon paper is black dye suspended in wax. Wax rubs off onto the white pages. Ants, mice, honeybees—they begin fading to black.

"The more you read it, the blacker they'll be," he says.

"They'll disappear," he says.

"*Funeral* is sort of my farewell to publishing," Phillips says. "I feel like I've done what I wanted to do with books.

"I feel like this every now and then," he says. "I get burned out. It takes a lot to make a book. It don't find a lot of writers I want to work with who want to work with me. I don't pay them. It takes a long time.

"A lot of my past titles are out of print. I sold out. I can't make more. I don't have the materials. Some I don't want to make anymore. They're too complicated. I made thirty copies of *Funeral*." A book made from copy paper, yet no two copies are alike. "When they're gone, they're gone."

I flip through *Funeral*. My fingertips turn black.

I look like I've been poisoned.

2006

HALLOWEEN ABC'S

A is for All Hallow's Eve, or Halloween. It starts at sunset on October 31—the night before All Hallows, or All Saints' Day, a day when Catholics celebrate those who have been beatified. All Souls' Day is the day after All Saints'. The church decreed it a day to pray for the recently departed, and those poor souls in purgatory: spirits still stalking the earth, not having earned entrance to Heaven. In the Middle Ages, the days were known collectively as Hallowtide. On the eve of All Souls', churches in Britain would ring bells, to scare away dead souls. Some churches rang bells all night long.

B is for Robert Burns, the Scottish poet. Burns wrote "Hallowe'en" in 1785. "Some merry, friendly, country-folks, / Together did convene, / To burn their nits, and pou their stocks, / And haud their Halloween." The poem refers to the Celtic Halloween custom of fortune-telling with nuts and apple peelings. Scots carried the custom to Canada. Other Halloween customs carried here by Scots and Irish: bonfires, begging for food door to door, playing pranks on those who would not furnish food.

C is for Caledonian Society. Founded in 1855 by affluent Scottish-Canadians, the Caledonian Society held banquets across Canada on Halloween. "We are not divining the future, or burning nuts, or catching the 'snap apple,' but celebrating Scottishness," a speaker told Caledonians in Montreal in 1885. In Toronto, George Brown was active in the Caledonians. Halloween here was a night of feasts: besides the Caledonian Society, the St. Andrew's society held a Halloween dinner, as did different regiments of the military, as did colleges at the University of Toronto. A meat market ran this ad on October 29, 1903: "Halloween Poultry. We are having enquiries already."

D is for the Dennison Manufacturing Co. "You would be surprised," said a young lady in *Bookseller & Stationer* magazine in 1924, "how many people give Hallowe'en parties the last two weeks of October." The young lady worked at a Toronto store. She supervised the crepe paper department. The Dennison Paper Manufacturing Co. of Framingham, Massachusetts was the country's main maker of crepe paper. Dennison opened a Toronto office in the early 1900s. It was located on Wellington St. W. They were the first to sell yellow, orange, and black crepe-paper. First to sell crepe paper printed with owls, bats, jack-o'-lanterns, black cats with arched backs. They published the *The Bogie Book*, the Bible of Halloween party guides. Place cards, centrepieces, Spanish moss, blindfolds, Jack Horner pies, pumpkin costumes—*The Bogie Book* told how to make them all from Dennison crepe paper. Crepe paper is combustible. The parties were fire traps.

E is for Eaton's. "Don't Miss the Hallowe'en Parade," read an Eaton's ad in the *Toronto Daily Star* in 1925. Eaton's Santa Claus Parade involved dozens of floats and hundreds of paraders. The Hallowe'en Parade? "A big pompous general will lead Felix and Bluebeard, a gypsy, a Zulu, and other familiar folks in a march around Toyland."

F is for Frankenstein. Billy Pratt was a British lad. In 1909, he was flunking out of King's College in London. He was studying Chinese customs and languages; he wanted to act. He sailed from Liverpool to Halifax, then wound his way to Toronto. The Canada Company office found him work in Hamilton. Pratt became a farmer. After three months, he drifted westward, working as a ditch digger, a tree cutter. In 1910, he convinced a stock company in Kamloops to let him perform in a play. He changed his name to Boris Karloff. Karloff was a surname of some of his relatives; Boris was a name, he said, that he "plucked out of the cold Canadian air." Karloff toured Alberta, Saskatchewan, Manitoba. Then he headed to Hollywood. His role as the monster in *Frankenstein* (1931) made him a star.

G is for ghost

H is for Dr. H. H. Holmes. In the 1880s, he built himself a building in Chicago that boasted, in the words of crime writer

Connie Fillipelli, "iron-plated rooms, secret passages, hidden chutes that ended in the basement directly above zinc-lined tanks, sealed rooms with gas jets, stairways that led nowhere...trapdoors, a dissecting table, surgeons' tools...." The building was a blueprint for every carnival and amusement park haunted house to come. It's believed Holmes murdered over a hundred bodies there. Then he went on the lam, landing in Toronto in 1892. He buried more bodies in the basement of a house near Barrie, Ontario. Pinkerton detectives shadowed him there. Again he fled. They nabbed him in Boston, tried him in Philadelphia. In 1896, he was hanged.

I is for Isabel Grace Mackenzie. She died in 1917, and was survived by her son, William Lyon Mackenzie King. Mackenzie King became the Prime Minister of Canada. He hung a portrait of Isabel in his study, and kept it lit night and day. He spoke to her through a Ouija board and a crystal ball. He contacted her during séances. On October 6, 1935, his dead mother communicated this to him through a medium: "Long ago I dreamt that you would succeed Sir Wilfrid Laurier. Long ago I knew God meant you to be Prime Minister. Long ago I [more than] knew that God meant that you would serve His holy will. Good night." He was buried beside his mother in Mt. Pleasant Cemetery. He was a Caledonian.

J is for jack-o'-lantern.

K is for kisses. "Ducking for apples is rather out of date," said the "Everywoman's Column" of the *Toronto Daily Star* in 1913. The topic: what games to have at a Halloween party. What did the column recommend? A taffy pull. "For the taffy pull, pull the taffy from buttered plates and save mother's busy hands next day." A taffy pull fulfilled two functions: it provided entertainment, and it provided eats. For hosts who didn't have time to cook candy, stores in Toronto sold it. At Halloween, a Canadian confectioner called Hunt's sold a "Taffy Sucker, Face on Stand" for a nickel. In 1925, Eaton's advertised a variety of taffies for Halloween: "peanut crisp, cocoanut and peanut, peanut and butterscotch." When the Depression took hold, Canadians couldn't afford sugar for taffy. They turned to molasses. The molasses kiss became the Halloween candy of choice. "Just in time for Hallowe'en parties," read an ad from Loblaw's in 1933, "Hallowe'en Kisses." Fifteen cents bought a one-pound bag.

L is for Bela Lugosi, the star of *Dracula* (1931). Dracula also made a movie star of David Manners, who played the handsome Jonathan Harker. Manners was born in Halifax. His real name: Rauff de Ryther Daun Acklom. For a time, he studied Forestry at the University of Toronto. He preferred to playact in the Little Theatre at Hart House. He hightailed it to Hollywood, where James Whale spotted him at a party. Whale cast him in his directorial debut, *Journey's End* (1930). Manners went on to work with directors Frank Capra and George Cukor. Tod Browning cast him in *Dracula*. In *The Mummy* (1932), Manners played opposite Boris Karloff. In *The Black Cat* (1934), he starred with both Bela Lugosi and Boris Karloff. When his studio suggested he marry a woman—Manners was gay—he abandoned movies for Broadway, where he mentored Marlon Brando. Retiring from acting, he retreated to the California desert. He wrote novels—several of them were best-sellers. He died in 1998. Horror movies, he once said, were his "only claim to movie fame."

M is for Philip Morris. In the 1950s, he toured across Canada performing in a ghost show, a magic show with supernatural and horrific effects. His stage name: Dr. Evil. To garner publicity, he'd arrive early in a town and pull stunts. Drive a car blindfolded. Raffle off a "dead body." The dead body was a frozen chicken. The RCMP once arrested him for dressing as a gorilla in public. Years later he invented an artificial spider web made of fabric. It made him a fortune. It is still being sold today.

N is for noise. In the nineteenth-century, making noise was at the heart of Halloween. Revellers tossed rocks and mud at windows and doors. They crafted noisemakers from tin cans, wooden spools, roofing tiles. A Halloween Package produced for Canadian school teachers in the 1940s includes instructions for making a Halloween megaphone. As early as 1900 Halloween noisemakers were being mass-produced in Germany for export to the U.S.A. Styles for sale included horns, rattles, cranks, snappers, and clappers. "Weird Spirits a-gamboling," said a 1913 ad for Mason & Risch, Limited of Yonge St. in Toronto. "Witch Caps—Pumpkin Heads—Dominoes—Flowing Robes—Holed-Out Eyes—Strange phantasies they are! Yes, WHO and WHAT are they? Listen, then, they are the phantom witcheries of Hallowe'en!" The ad was peddling the Victor Victrola. "To sit snugly around the open fire, reveling in all the mystic rhythms of this bewitching fairyland of Hallowe'en, conjured up so wonderfully by the little Victrola …." Which mystic rhythms did the store recommend? "The Dance o' the Fairies," "Peer Gynt," and "Will-of-the-Wisp."

O is for owl.

J is for Johnston & McFarlane. Germans were the first to mass-produce pranks. A German toy catalogue from 1751 contains smoke powder, chemical blood, trick spiders, and mechanical bugs. Canadian toy stores started importing German gags in the late nineteenth century. Johnston & McFarlane of Yonge St. supplied Toronto. "[A] wealth of baffling conjuring tricks, brain tests and mind reading, chemical and physical magic, magnetism, candy-making, parlour games, etc., etc.," is how the firm once described its stock. Arthur E. McFarlane was also an author. He wrote essays, a crime novel, and *Redney McGraw*, a novella about a newsie who becomes a circus hand. A Johnston & McFarlane ad from 1899 offers an Imp bottle, a Trick Box, a Laughing Camera, and a What-is-it, "a most comical surprise … the greatest fun maker out." The What-is-it was a toy lizard.

Q is for Kew Beach. In 1945, Halloween hooligans burnt bonfires on Queen Street East. To feed the fire, they tore down fences and gates and scavenged construction sites. Police were called. When they rode up on horses, they were pelted with stones and bricks. Hooligans blocked fire trucks with piles of concrete blocks. Thirteen troublemakers were taken in. A mob of 7,000 or so marched on the police station on Main Street, hell-bent on springing the hooligans. Police cruisers rushed to the scene with tear gas. Water cannons dispersed rioters. Five firemen were injured, as were a couple of cops.

R is for rides. Leon Cassidy needed a dark ride. In 1928, Cassidy was co-owner of a small amusement park in New Jersey. Most amusement parks had an Old Mill ride: boats floated riders down water canals decorated with scary scenery and strange sounds. Cassidy couldn't afford to build a boat ride. So he put dodge-'em cars on a twisted track in a darkened pavilion. The Pretzel, he called it. It was a sensation.

He started the Pretzel Amusement Ride, Co. to provide pretzel rides to amusement parks across the continent. In 1930, he came to Canada. He put down a plywood base at the Canadian National Exhibition. He attached tracks to the base, then covered them in a black tent, then covered the black tent in another tent. It was the first cartable dark ride on any midway anywhere.

S is for slogans. Trick or treat! It's what children scream on Halloween. But trick or treat didn't become the customary catchphrase in Toronto until after World War Two. Before then, kids yelled, "Shell out!" "Hallowe'en," said an ad for a Toronto grocery store chain in 1929, "with its joyous merriment … SHELLIN' OUT to the district cut-ups, guessing who the strange figure is who knocks on your door." From a Loblaw's ad during the Depression: "When you hear the ultimatum! SHELL OUT! Be ready with Loblaw's Hallowe'en Kisses."

T is for Bill Tracy, a sculptor and engineer from New Jersey. In the 1950s, he revolutionized carnival dark rides by adding supernatural back-glows, glow-in-the dark stunts, *trompe l'oeil* to the decor. He created themed rides like the western ghost town and the haunted pirate ship. Sadly, he never invented safety features, like fire escapes. Wiring was makeshift. His rides tended to go up in flames. Very few still stand. The dark ride at Toronto's Centreville Park—the Haunted Barrel—is decorated in a distinctly Tracy mode. And it is safe.

U is for the University of Toronto. According to historian Keith Walden, spontaneous Halloween celebrations erupted on campus in 1884. Students marched into the downtown core, singing, shattering lampposts, egging Eaton's. Police dispersed them. Torontonians complained. The parade became an annual event. In 1899 students barged into the peanut gallery at Massey Hall, disrupting the evening's performance. Veterinary students dangled dead horse parts over the balcony. Medical students banged human arm and leg bones. Some students slit open a political effigy, showering the audience below with chaff, hay, and excelsior. Hector Charlesworth, future editor of *Saturday Night*, was sitting in the pit. His suit was ruined.

V is for vampire.

W is for whoopie cushion. In the early decades of the twentieth century, an American named S.S. Adams invented a plethora of classic pranks: dribble glasses, joy buzzers, fake dog doo-doo. In 1930, a Canadian "rubber concern" approached him with a new novelty—a bladder that made a farting sound when someone sat on it. The rubber concern? The JEM Rubber Co. It was headquartered on Dundas St. W.

It produced parts for printing companies. In the late 1920s, it molded an inflatable bag that farted. Adams refused the fart cushion, JEM manufactured it on its own. It was green, with a wooden nozzle. Stamped on the face was a picture of a Scottish lad. He sported spurs and a sporran, and carried a rifle. Wouldn't bagpipes have been the obvious visual pun? The whoopee cushion was a sensation, even during the Depression. Hundreds of thousands sold. Adams ended up coming out with a copy of the Canadian cushion—the Razzberry Cushion, he called it.

X is for XEPN, a radio station near the Rio Grande. In the 1920s, Bob Nelson and his brother Larry hosted an astrology show on the station. Listeners sent in a dollar; in return, the Nelsons sent them a mimeographed horoscope. The Nelsons also operated Nelson Enterprises of Columbus, Ohio, which supplied mediums and mentalists in the United States and Canada with fake fortune telling equipment — mindreading codes, mechanical crystal balls, two-way radios that could be concealed under capes or in turbans. "Be it distinctly understood," said their 1931 mail-order catalogue, "that all effects described in this catalogue are accomplished by normal means, and are entirely divorced from any supernatural or supernormal powers .... "

Y is for yellow. "Green and red have come to be the Christmas colours," said a newspaper article from 1925, "just as black and yellow tell us of Hallowe'en." An article in *Bookseller & Stationer* in 1925 advised those celebrating Halloween to obtain "yellow and black crepe paper for decorative purposes." In 1927, an ad for crepe paper in that same magazine recommended "Orange and Black for Hallowe'en." In coming years, orange and black would come to be the Halloween palette par excellence. Yellow? What became of yellow?

Z is for zombies.

2008

WHAT SANTA WEARS AT HALLOWEEN

"Since the Puritan distrust of this great feast day abated, the American people ... have taken up Christmas with the same enthusiasm that lately almost buried funerals under a weight of floral tributes."

The editorial was published in the *Manitoba Daily Free Press* in December, 1886. Christmas is too commercial, the unnamed editorialist laments. Shopping, he believes, has become the *raison d'être* of the holiday, which, in its present state, will be worn out in little more than a decade.

"We readily incline to excess," he writes, "to an excess that destroys the object we seek."

Critiques of commercialism are a holiday tradition, as customary as caroling and candy canes. If it's not commercialism, it's something else: Santa Claus is the Devil, Santa is damaging children's psychologies, the pressure to shop for Christmas presents is forcing men to do what is properly women's work. Defenders of Christmas include both Christians and non-Christians; or, as the *New York Times* once put it, "[t]he corruption of Christmas has been roundly decried by everyone, whether they shop at Bloomingdale's or Wal-Mart."

Christmas is always about to be corrupted; the faithful are always decrying its corruption. I myself attempted to corrupt it.

I did it in the name of Halloween.

"Merry Christmas!" I yelled. "Merry Christmas!"

When I was six, I was an elf. I was in the Santa Claus Parade in Peterborough, Ontario, my hometown. I was standing on the final float, Santa's float, with other elves.

The float in front of us was Alice's Adventures in Wonderland. The Jack of Hearts was played by a boy a tad older than me. He was beautiful. I waved to him. During the course of the parade, I developed a crush on him. If it wasn't my first crush, it was pretty close to it. I didn't tell anybody about it. I knew there was something monstrous about liking a boy. It made me monstrous.

Halloween was more my style.

I don't associate homosexuality with Halloween; I do, however, associate my homosexuality with Halloween.

As a boy, I went trick or treating as a witch. I went as a skeleton. I was Dracula. Since I felt like a monster, why not be a monster whom others feared? On my dresser I had a Dracula model kit. On my bookshelf I had a werewolf mask which I kept beside werewolf books, *The Wolf Man* and *The Werewolf of London*. A poster of Lon Chaney, the Man of a Thousand Faces, was tacked on my wall. I had read all about him, about the pains he took to distort and disguise his body.

There's such a thing as loving monsters too much, a friend of my family's once said to my Mom while I was around.

If our house was haunted, it was haunted by me.

If I was haunted by Halloween, then my parents were haunted by Christmas. When I was growing up, my folks ran a small department store in a town near Peterborough. In winter the store was dead. In summer it came alive with cottagers and tourists. The fall brought back to school shoppers and Halloween. Candy sales soared.

The period between Halloween and Christmas was what mattered most. That's when we counted on making most of our money. Would it be good? We fretted. We feared. We decorated. Several times a year, the family would take a shopping trip to a display dealer in Toronto. For Halloween, we bought strangely large spiders and spider webs. For Christmas, there were giant glass balls and sparkling Styrofoam snowflakes. Everything scaled to parade float size. We would dress our store's windows with them. They had a magic effect on customers—they made them sentimental, nostalgic. Made them spend money.

The snowflakes were spider webs spray-painted white.

Years later, as an adult, I wrote a book called *Christmas Days* about the history of Christmas in Canada. It focused on the material culture of the season, the stuff that made Christmas Christmas.

Fake snow, I wrote, had once been created by crushing glass; later, it was made with asbestos. Christmas Crackers had once contained enough gunpowder to set fire to a table.

My book was full of fire. Christmas trees lit with candles burned up. Santa Claus costumes made of cheap cotton and crepe paper burned up if a sleeve so much as grazed a candle.

Santa Claus parades were perilous, too. Santa froze on his sleigh. Floats plowed into overpasses and telephone wires. An incorrectly constructed float could trap carbon dioxide in the driver's cab. An exhaust pipe could become as hot as a blowtorch.

Was I relishing the macabre a bit too much? Probably. I was playing the perverse elf I had been as a boy. I was perverting the holiday. I was Halloweening it. What I was doing was nothing new: making Christmas macabre is a Christmas tradition as old as Santa Claus.

Edinburgh Dungeon is a tourist trap in the shadow of Edinburgh Castle in Scotland. It features a labyrinth, a waxworks torture chamber, and what carnival workers call dark rides: rides such as haunted houses or tunnels of love that operate by and large in blackness.

In 2001, the Dungeon added a Christmas attraction, Satan's Grotto. An actor disguised as Satan sat on a throne while Santa Claus boiled in a witch's cauldron nearby. Santa's elves were dead, impaled on spikes. Robins roasted on an open fire.

"We don't mean to offend anyone," the manager of Satan's Grotto told the press. "It's just a bit of welcome relief from something much more scary ... the Christmas shopping."

Who wants to Halloween Christmas? There are those who find Christmas saccharine. There are those who find it maddeningly maudlin. There are those for whom Christmas is an endless to-do list of shopping and working. There are those who feel obligated to give gifts to people they despise. There are those who are lonely at Christmas. There are those for whom Christmas brings back miserable memories of Christmases past. There are those like me who hated being dragged to Christmas service at churches full of pious pricks. The Christmas season bedevils many of us; many of us like to see the season bedeviled back.

Mischief and the macabre are hallmarks of Halloween. At Halloween, they're the usual. At Christmas, they're unusual and often cruel.

Santa Claus bears the brunt of the cruelty. As Christmas's eminence, he is eminently corruptible, which is why he's the star of so many sinister stories. In some of the stories, he's depicted as a monster; in others, he's a sweet elf who's been supplanted by an impostor, a frightening fraud.

A Trap for Santa Claus, directed by D.W. Griffith in 1907, shows children setting a trap in a fireplace on Christmas Eve. When Santa comes down the chimney—or rather, when the children's deadbeat dad comes down the chimney to rob them—he's snared.

In Dr. Seuss's 1957 storybook *How the Grinch Stole Christmas!*, Santa isn't Santa: he's a monster. Dressed in a Santa hat and coat, he steals into houses in Whoville and then steals the presents piled under the Whos' Christmas trees. A monster has no trouble stealing into houses; what does that say about Santa?

In a 1953 number of *Panic*, a comic magazine from the minds behind *Mad*, Santa is seen sliding down a chimney and into a bear trap set by a surly child. It's tough to say if he's an impostor: though he rode in on a sleigh, he's sporting a beard that has a "100% wool" label stuck to it. Stuck to his sleigh is a sign that says "Just Divorced." Dangling from the sleigh: a cleaver, a carving knife and the lid of a garbage can.

Sinister Christmas stories always pose these questions: Will Christmas survive? Will we survive Christmas?

In 1991, Tim Burton released his animated movie *The Nightmare Before Christmas*. It tells the tale of Jack Skellington, a skeleton from Halloween Town, who stumbles into Christmas Town and becomes fascinated by it. Desperate to understand the holiday, he spirits Santa Claus to Halloween Town and takes over his yuletide duties. He finds, though, that where Santa once spread fun, he only spreads fear and revulsion.

The Nightmare before Christmas is the most famous fable of Halloween corrupting Christmas; it is far from my favourite.

Halloween is a time for mischief. Jack Skellington commits his mischief unwittingly. How is that fun?

Halloween is a time for villainy. When Jack Skellington returns to Halloween Town, he reunites with his sweetheart, a glorified ragdoll. It's supposedly romantic.

The film's music is meretricious. What's worse, the film itself is a conceptual failure. Here's why: Halloween can be as saccharine as Christmas. And Christmas? It can't be Halloweened. It was corrupted by Halloween a long time ago.

Halloween bleeds into Christmas, Christmas creeps into Halloween: it's always been this way.

In the late 1990s, I went to Toronto's Santa Claus Parade. I had been to it a bunch of times as a child. It was as I remembered. There were clowns. There were marching bands.

What was new: a haunted house.

It was purple and black. A skeletal tree stood beside it. Sounds of screams and clanking chains came from the windows.

It was a float. It was built of wood and lath. The tree was I don't know what—a real tree spray painted black? Ringing the house were witches and ghosts—or children in witch and ghost costumes.

Spectators didn't know what to do. Kids didn't wave at it. They didn't cheer. What would they have been cheering for? Nightmares? Parents pooh-poohed it. They didn't mind garish floats, but a ghoulish float? I didn't understand their shock. The haunted house is the icon par excellence of both Christmas and Halloween, though the forces that infest it have shifted in time.

"[T]he feast of Christ's nativity is attended with such profaneness, as that it deserves the name of Saturn's Mass, or of Bacchus his mass, or if you will, the Devil's Mass .... "

So said Increase Mather in 1767. Puritans spurned Christmas. In 17th century New England, it was illegal to celebrate it. Fines were imposed on any persons "found observing any such day as Xmas or the like ..." Mather stated that since it could not be proved that Christ was born on December 25, the holiday was a heresy. Celebrating it was blasphemous.

Mather had a point. Christmas celebrations back then looked like Halloween celebrations do today. There was drunkenness. Revelers marched in mock-parades and made as much noise as possible. The poor and the downtrodden knocked on the doors of the wealthy and powerful. They demanded money. They demanded food.

There were costumes. Men dressed as women. Mummers in masks paraded down streets, stopping in at houses to surprise the residents. Some mummers sat in spooky silence, refusing to say who they were. Some mummers put on skits. All mummers expected hospitality, and they received it.

Increase Mather decried the celebration of Christmastide; so, too, did he decry Hallowtide. All Saints' and All Souls' Days—Hallowtide, they were collectively called—were well-established by the end of the 12th century. The church decreed that on these days—November 1 and 2—the living would pray for the saints and for the souls of the departed.

Halloween—the eve of Hallowtide—was fraught with folk beliefs. It was considered supernatural, a time when nothing separated the underworld from our world; nothing but wind. Goblins gallivanted. Ghosts went about. Witches were abroad. Frightened folks built bonfires to frighten away the forces of evil. Churches in Britain would ring bells. Some churches rang bells all night long.

It is impossible to say what the Puritans thought of Santa Claus; he hadn't been invented yet.

Clement Clarke Moore was the son of Benjamin Moore, the Episcopalian Bishop of New York. By the 1800s, Episcopalians were celebrating Christmas at Church. So, too, were Unitarians. And Methodists. The time of Puritan rule had passed. It had become acceptable to observe Christmas.

"[T]here existed no Christmas rituals that were socially acceptable to the upper class," writes Christmas scholar

Stephen Nissenbaum about the 1820s in New York. Since Clement Clarke Moore was upper class, Christmas day would have entailed churchgoing and religious reflection.

For the lower classes, the day was different. As a newspaper of the period put it, it entailed roaming "the streets all night, disturbing the slumbers of the weary … by thumping upon tin kettles, sounding penny [whistles] and other martial trumpets." It was noisy. It was a nuisance. The upper class longed to see misrule ruled out, to see hooliganism replaced by genteel rituals, to see a new conception of Christmas created in the United States.

So Moore composed a poem.

In *A Visit from St. Nicholas*, a father is startled from sleep when St. Nick arrives at his house on Christmas Eve. He watches him slip silently down the chimney and into the drawing room; watches him fill stockings with toys; watches him fly away on his sleigh. The poem was simple enough that parents could recite it to children. It made implicit that Christmas was to be a night for the dreams of children to come true—the silent dreams.

Who was St. Nick? He was a Dutch folk figure. He'd been a character in Washington Irving's 1819 book *Knickerbocker's History of New York*, portrayed as "the mythic patron saint of New Amsterdam," to borrow a phrase from Nissenbaum. Irving's book purported to be a history of New Amsterdam in old Dutch times, but it was not; Irving depicted St. Nick as being an important part of that history, though he was not.

He had a saint's wagon. He smoked a pipe. In a particular passage, he was seen "laying his finger beside his nose." In St. Nicholas, Irving took a minor figure from the past and endowed him with wisdom, wit, goodness and, most importantly, with cultural importance. Moore nicked St. Nick for *A Visit from St. Nicholas* and turned him into Santa Claus, who would in time turn into a cultural icon, a poetic creation who seemed to have been around forever.

How did Halloween corrupt into this new conception of Christmas? Instead of being an immortal saint, as St. Nicholas had been, Santa Claus was a supernatural creature, an eternal elf who crept into homes on the same night each year. He was Halloween in Christmas costume.

It's said that Santa stops at every house in the world; if that's so, then every house is haunted.

"Why do you come, to haunt me so?" the actor says.

It's Christmas Eve, 1863. A Christmas play's being performed: *The Haunted Man and the Ghost's Bargain*.

The play's based on the book by Charles Dickens, the fifth of his Christmas-themed titles. It features a miserable man who is visited by a spectre on Christmas Eve.

"I see you in the fire," the actor declaims, "I hear you in music, in the wind, in the dead stillness of night!" The actor is playing the haunted man. As he speaks, something appears onstage. Is it light? Is it a man? It is a man made of light—he has a voice, he has a visage, he is visible, but barely. He is see-through.

The play was performed in London. The ghost was the creation of a professor at the University, John Pepper. Using an optical technique he called Pepper's Ghost, he produced a transparent ghost upon the stage—the ghost acted real, the ghost looked real, and it glowed. Here's how he did it: mirrors. The image of an actor garbed as a ghost was reflected onto a pane of glass on the stage. The audience didn't see the glass; they saw a glowing ghost, clanking across the boards, ghost chains clamped to his ghost ankles.

Pepper's Ghost wasn't created explicitly for the Dickens play, but the play was the perfect way to showcase it. Pepper took it on a theatrical tour of the United States. After seeing a performance of it, P.T. Barnum stole it for the sideshow he called his museum. At Barnum's American Museum on Broadway, patrons paid to see General Tom Thumb, bearded ladies and tattooed men. He put a ghost on display. So real was it, he claimed, that certain customers shot pistols at it. They missed.

Santa Claus haunts homes at Christmas; Halloween haunts homes in October, and all year round at carnivals.

Haunted houses, the sort made for fun and profit, date back to Barnum's day and to the birth of the American amusement park.

In 1902, the Old Mill ride opened at Sea Lion Park at Coney Island. It looked like a water-driven mill. Water churned by a waterwheel wound through a circuit of shallow canals. Brave riders drifted in boats. The canals carried them through dark tunnels decorated to look like scary caves. Grotesque things greeted them: clown faces, dancing devil dolls, and, sometimes, taxidermied animals.

By 1905, Coney Island was crawling with amusement parks—Steeplechase, Luna Park, Dreamland—and the amusement parks were crawling with dark rides. Coney Hell's Gate at Dreamland took boat riders through a series of supernatural grottos. In 1908, the London Ghost Show was making big money at the nearby Brighton Beach Park. Its secret: Pepper's Ghost.

In the summer, carnies had Coney Island; come winter, they had Santalands, which is what department and dry goods stores called their toy departments at Christmastime.

In the late 19th century, department stores started to hire Santas to staff their Santalands. They found them at the bottom of the show biz barrel: carnies, clowns, and out-of-work vaudevillians.

The carnies did what carnies do: they put on a ballyhoo. A ballyhoo is a free act intended to draw crowds. Santas did magic tricks. Santas showed off animal acts, bears that played banjos, bears that danced with dogs. Anteaters.

The earliest Santalands looked like the earliest haunted attractions. Santa would stand in a grotto sculpted from papier-mâché, or in a cave painted to look like ice. Icicles dangled down. Icicles of cotton and glycerine.

By the Great Depression, stores were advertising Coney Island-style attractions in their stores. Miniature trains carried children through stockrooms painted to depict the North Pole or Candyland. Christmassy content was not a requirement. Simpsons in Montreal installed a pirate-themed attraction for the holidays. What says Christmas like cutlasses and pantaloons?

The Messmore & Damon Company of New York City specialized in papier-mâché. Department stores bought their urns, which resembled marble.

In the 1910s the company, consisting of George Herold Messmore and Joseph Damon, found fortune building parade floats. The Santa Claus Parade in Toronto was a client, as was the Macy's Thanksgiving Day parade in New York.

From floats they turned to Santalands, which they

revolutionized. Their mechanized Santas made it possible for department stores to do away with live acts that better belonged in dime museums.

When they weren't making Christmas dreams come true, they were scaring the pants off of people. At Coney Island, they constructed a History of Torture, in which human-like mannequins got burned, flogged and murdered in an Iron Maiden. They continued to design dark rides well into the 1960s.

I am a member of D.A.F.E., Darkride and Funhouse Enthusiasts. I collect and covet relics from Messmore & Damon's Company's career. I have a haunted house catalogue of theirs from the late 1960s. For sale: stunts to decorate a dark ride. Satan "moves his arms and turns his head." Yours for $595.

The haunted house that I saw at the Santa Claus Parade in the 1990s reminded me of a carnival dark ride.

It was the design: walls all different sizes, a rickety roof that sloped here and rose there. It looked like a Whacky Shack by Bill Tracy, a great dark ride designer of the 1960s.

The difference was that in a Bill Tracy ride, a rider sits while a car whisks him along his way. At the parade, the ride was whisking by us. Was the street its course? Were the streetcar tracks its tracks? It's a trick. If Santa Claus turns every house in a haunted house, then the haunted house float turns us all into dark ride décor: we're the skeletons that spring from walls, the vampires that dead fall from trapdoors, the devils that move our arms and turn our heads.

While writing this essay, I spoke to a float builder who's been working for the parade for decades. He remembers haunted house floats from the 1980s and 1990s. Kids hid inside them. They held ghost cut-outs that were nailed to poles. As the parade proceeded, they stuck the ghosts through the windows and shook them. He told me that there might yet be some ghosts lying around the workshop.

There were plenty of people, he said, who were bothered by those floats, who felt ghosts and goblins didn't belong in the parade.

He told me a story. The Santa Claus Parade is always staged on a Sunday. Sometime in the 1980s, it was held on Sunday, November 1. As parade-goers gathered to greet Santa, Halloween partiers were still straggling home. Jack-o'-lanterns lay smashed on the street. The mayor of Toronto called the parade offices to complain. You can't have a parade at that time, the mayor said. Halloween is too close. It's too close.

2011

THE DYING PIG

FRIGHT THIS WAY.

The Grim Reaper looms over everything, in one arm a scythe, in the other a sign: *FRIGHT THIS WAY.*

The reaper's an inflatable. He's surrounded by inflatables: vampires, zombies, and psychopathic clowns.

There's an inflatable skeleton. There's an inflatable skeleton in an inflatable coffin. An inflatable tombstone bears the inscription: *HERE LIES WILLIE B. BACK.* For francophones, there's another inscription on the other side: *CI-GIT G. RENDULAM.*

Happy Halloween! It's the season when stores are stocked with decorations of the dead and dying. It's the season when stores are stocked with inflatables of the dead and the dying.

They could sell an inflatable of me:

I'm dying.

Insufflation.

It's medical. It's the act of blowing a substance—powder, air, medicine—into the orifice of a body.

I've had it done to me many times—doctors puff air up my ass so that my rectum and colon puff out, then they look for cancer.

That is, they look for more cancer.

It's a painful process, but pleasurable, too—while I'm inflated, I like to think I've become something besides myself—an inflatable.

I have not seen myself being insufflated—my head's always down, my ass up. I'm told that it can be done manually—a doctor pumps air into my rectum with a bladder. What goes in is room air; what comes out is something else. I'm told that it can be done automatically—an insufflating contraption pumps CO_2 into my rectum. What inflatables have is similar—an electric fan puffs them up from the inside as soon as it's plugged in. When I'm puffed up, I could rupture. When they're puffed up, they could rupture—they are, after all, balloons.

At Halloween, balloons are the ideal décor—they're so good at death.

"The Importance of Hallowe'en Trade"—this was a headline in a stationery trade magazine in 1916. "Masks, lanterns, favors, and place cards, besides post cards and other novelties, can all be sold most readily for Hallowe'en."

Balloons were novelties.

Halloween balloons were much the same then as now—black and orange stamped with skulls and skeletons. The rubber was heavier. The dye on the rubber rubbed off. They had trumpet ends: when air went out, they wailed.

"Fun For All!" read a headline in the same trade magazine in 1922. The big seller was "The Broadway Chicken"—a balloon in a costume.

The chicken was a yellow balloon with a cardboard beak and yellow feathers glued to it. When it deflated, it squawked. Another company offered "The Dying Pig," a balloon with ears and legs stuck to it. It screamed like a slaughterhouse as air shot out its asshole.

All assholes are trumpet ends.

In 1945, a jack-o'-lantern floated down Columbus Avenue.

It was a balloon in Macy's Thanksgiving Day Parade in New York City. Why put a jack-o'-lantern in a Thanksgiving parade?

Why not?

The first Macy's parade took place in 1924. The floats were trucks decorated with crepe paper and costumed characters.

Then, in 1927, it got balloons. They were floats that floated. They were stories high—they peered into fortieth-floor apartments.

Tony Sarg, a puppeteer, designed them. That first year he did a Felix the Cat, a floppy-eared elephant, and a dragon. A team of the store's employees held them aloft with poles. The balloons were rubberized silk pumped up with oxygen. The following year, Sarg pumped helium into them. At the end of the parade, the employees let them soar up into the sky. There they expanded, then exploded.

Felix's skin fell onto the street. An ear, an eye, an asshole.

In 1929, Sarg built the balloons with slow-release valves—when the balloons were let go, they propelled themselves across the city. The balloons alit in the Bronx, in Brooklyn. They didn't make it to Toronto, though Toronto had balloons of its own. The Santa Claus Parade tried them out in the 1930s. It didn't try helium. They would have died on streets here—snagged on railway bridges, electrocuted on streetcar cables.

Balloons are born to die.

How do inflatables die? There are storms—winds whip them away. There's vandalism—shootings, stabbings, slashings. A penknife can waste a werewolf. A garden stake can take down a vampire. Then there's wear and tear. Air fans fail. Seams pull apart. Sunlight fades the fabric till it's brittle—you can't put a vampire in the sun for too long. He'll bleed out, bow down, then drop to the ground. Then he's nothing. He's a tree skirt.

When I die, I like to think it'll be with a bang—a desufflation of gas, shit, lube, like a balloon that's been buttfucked or a butt that's been balloon-fucked—the dying pig as dying fag.

2017

THE SHIT NECKLACE

Shit.

Judy Blame is dead.

Blame was a brilliant jeweler of the punk era.

Some of his jewelry was shit.

There's a photo I love: Blame in a Blame, a necklace made of shit, a bib necklace featuring fake turds cascading down his chest.

This is what fashion calls a statement piece. What was the statement? That fashion is shit? That shit is fashion?

Who would say such a thing?

Le Shit?

The Shit?

What was that necklace called?

Fake shit is funny. It doesn't look like shit. It looks like something that's trying to look like shit.

Judy Blame's necklace wasn't jewelry. It was something that looked like joke jewelry. A fuck you to fakeness. A fuck you from fakeness.

Wasn't that what punk was?

Whatever Judy Blame did—he made jewelry, yes, but he also styled shoots, singers, and fashion shows—was magic to me.

I've been a fan forever, since finding his work in the magazines that I memorized as a teenager: *The Face, i-D, Blitz*.

He was a punk, which is what I wanted to be. He was a jeweler, which I wanted to be. He was a faggot. I am a faggot too, though I think he was better at it.

I wanted to be his kind of punk, but had to settle for writing. I think of words as brooches pinned to paper. I think of sentences as shit necklaces.

There are fourteen turds in this sentence.

So this story's for Judy.

In 1977, the year of the Silver Jubilee, the year the Sex Pistols got busted playing on a boat on the Thames, he was seventeen and squatting in London.

He wore the clothes that punks wore: He went down to Seditionaries and bought bondage pants.

He wore the jewelry that punks wore: safety pins, zippers, badges. He stuck them to his clothes. He stuck them to his body. He wrapped a zipper around his head. It made him look like he'd had a new brain put in.

Like Vivienne Westwood was his surgeon.

Punk created Judy Blame. He created punk, too.

He took its tropes and twisted them, then twisted them some more.

He screen-printed safety pins onto badges. He bound badges in tartan, and then speared them with safety pins.

He mudlarked. It sounds scatological. It means he rummaged for treasures in riverbanks, especially the banks of the Thames. The treasures—bones, bottle caps, broken bits of crockery—he transformed into finery: *bijoux de la boue*.

Toys, charms, pinchbeck chains: he collected all sorts of crap. He combined it in beautiful *objets* that he wore when he went clubbing, or to tea. It didn't matter what it was—a newspaper headdress, or cutlery tucked into a hatband, or a cap so encrusted with buttons and beads that it looks like memory ware—he looked brilliant, like nothing before him.

He looked like Judy Blame.

He made jewelry for himself to wear. He made it for his friends to wear. Sometimes he sold some.

In the mid-1980s, he co-founded House of Beauty and Culture alongside designer Christopher Nemeth and shoemaker John Moore and more.

It was a cult store: not easy to find, not easy to find open.

The people who went paid mind to what was in it.

Jean Paul Gaultier came, as did his assistant, Martin Margiela.

Blame's salvaged style—a brooch might be a high heel with a pin glued to it—would come to be called Deconstruction when Margiela developed it in his own classic collections.

With time, the whole fashion world would come calling on Blame. In 2005, Rei Kawakubo commissioned jewelry for the boys in Comme des Garçons's Homme Plus collection; he came up with brooches of gold chain and fluorescent pink plastic soldiers. In the following decade came collaborations with Kim Jones at Louis Vuitton, Marc Jacobs, Paco Rabanne.

I don't know why none of those designers did an edition of the shit necklace.

A few years ago, doctors discovered cancer in me. I had surgeries. I had therapies. I spent a lot of time in bed, and a lot of time shitting.

I did both at the same time sometimes.

Instagram was a wonderful waste of time. I followed Judy. He posted pictures of his work, pictures of his world, pictures that annoyed or amused him.

I posted a picture of him in his shit necklace. He liked it.

After my cancer, the necklace seemed—well, not serious, but more serious. It was still funny, but also fearsome; still sickening, but also sickly. The turds are mostly the same shape: swirly. They're all different consistencies and colors—a brown, a yellow-brown, an orange-brown—that shit shouldn't necessarily be.

The necklace is a symptom of something.

When I heard that Blame had died of cancer-related causes, another of his masterworks came to mind.

It's a necklace made from chain, a set of brass knuckles, and a pair of plastic skeleton claws that seem to be grabbing at a cigarette that dangles between them.

Who turns a burning fag into a piece of a parure?

Jewelry is anything—this was part of his proposition. The other part was this: everything is jewelry.

What does this mean?

It means the cigarette he smoked was jewelry; his lips wore it. The cigarette smoke was jewelry; his lungs wore it. The cancer was jewelry; his body wore it.

Is it too much to say that cancer's something you wear?

I'll say this: it wears you out.

2018

GAY FLOU

When is a fashion show a funeral? When it's Jean Paul
Gaultier. Take his final couture presentation: it was a sort of
death, or a spoof of death, or a spoof of spoofs of death.

It put the poof in spoof.

Gaultier started the show with a funeral. The stage was filled
with models in mourning black. Pallbearers in black veils
carried a coffin on the stage. It wasn't clear what had died.
Fashion itself? Do styles ever die, or do they come back
undead and undeader?

When the coffin opened, a model in a babydoll dress strutted
out and started the show. What followed was a lesson in what
to wear to funerals. Among the suggestions: rooster feathers,
inflatable cone bras, sponges stitched together into skirts.
There were camouflage gowns sewn from tons of tulle. They
signaled a grand idea: that fashion could camouflage you from
death. He could have gone further with it: Why not wear
grave dirt?

The inside lid of the coffin was as shiny as a mirror: a coffin-
cum-changeroom. Death, he seemed to be saying, isn't the
end: it's just a different look

Death has always stalked Gaultier's *defilés*. It's done so in the
figure of the sailor. The sailor can be a man, it can be a woman,
it can be something that's neither nor. It can be Gaultier
himself. It often appears in a *marinière*, a Breton-striped sailor

sweater, *matelot* pants with a fall front, and perhaps a sailor's cap with a red pompom: *le pompom funèbre*.

This sailor comes largely from French literature: it was there in Jean Lorrain; it was there in Cocteau; and it was there in Genet—the gayest sailor of all was Querelle.

"Querelle," Gaultier once told an interviewer, "is the ultimate sailor, a hypersexualized gay symbol, a fantasy, an icon, a form of virility that could be ambiguous." I might also mention that Querelle was murderous—virility and violence in a beefy body.

The Genetian sailor was constant in Gaultier's career. Gaultier put him on catwalks and in commercials with other characters that complemented him: Existentialists, accordionists, circus acts, burlesquers. To paraphrase *The Thief's Journal*: they all belonged to the region of himself which he called Paris.

Paris was his dream. He grew up in the suburbs of the city: he learned about it by studying magazines and by watching TV. It was TV that showed him the Folies Bergère. It showed him *Falbalas* (1945), the film that made him dream of fashion design. It showed him "Dim Dom Dam," the magazine program that introduced him to Coco Chanel, Saint Laurent, as well as writers in Genet's gang: Sartre, de Beauvoir, Violette Leduc.

In 1970, at age seventeen, Gaultier went to work for Pierre Cardin. He hadn't studied fashion formally; he'd taught himself to sketch, and his sketches impressed Cardin. He presented his first prêt-a-porter show in 1978; it wasn't until 1982, though, that critics noticed him. Gays like me loved him straightaway: he was the only designer who showed men and women in similarly sexy styles. In 1985, he did a menswear show and it was gay as fuck: men in skirts, men in backless sweaters, men in chiffon, lace and all the soft fabrics that couturiers call *le flou*.

It rhymes with marabou.

The 1980s belonged to Gaultier. In those years, it seemed that the *New York Times* couldn't let a week go by without mentioning his clothes or who was wearing them or where to buy them. What the *Times* didn't mention was the word gay: Gaultier was outrageous, offensive, an *enfant terrible*, but not gay; his designs were totally unwearable, wild, weird, wiggy, androgynous, but not gay. The *Times*—and the popular fashion press—found him fascinating, if too froufrou; God forfend it say he was a faggot. God forfend it say what was happening with faggots and AIDS.

When Gaultier's lover and business partner, Francis Menuge, died of AIDS in 1990, Gaultier almost gave up. It had been a dream of theirs to found their own couture house. Gaultier did it alone in 1997; he named it Gaultier Paris. He continued to present some of the same silhouettes he'd been designing for so long. He executed them in the most expensive fabrics and with the expertise of some of the world's most talented seamstresses. Still, some critics considered it all a case of déjà-vu. Me, I like to think that Gaultier was in a dream he'd dreamed with Menuge: though he couldn't bring him back, his *vêtements* could be *revenants*.

And he went out with a bang. The show boasted one of his most macabre ensembles: a black tuxedo jacket, *le smoking*, with a funeral wreath strapped on the back. It's the perfect accessory—no matter where you drop dead, no matter when, no matter how, you already have a tribute, an immortelle with this motto spelled out across the sash: *La Mode Pour La Vie*.

2020

GOTH IS DEAD

Gothic is back. Gothic is black.

"Black is certainly the gothic color *par excellence*," writes famed fashion historian Valerie Steele in *Gothic: Dark Glamour*. The book was recently published to accompany an exhibit of the same name that Steele curated at the Museum at the Fashion Institute of Technology in New York City.

Black, black, black—*Gothic: Dark Glamour* is chock-a-block with black. There are black dresses by Galliano, Givenchy, Gareth Pugh. There are black dresses by designer Ann Demeulemeester, the so-called "Dark Queen of Belgian Fashion." There are mourning dresses and jet jewelry from Victorian days. Even the endpapers are black.

But beware! "[N]ot all black clothes are gothic," Steele says, "nor are all gothic fashions black." Gothic is more than a colour; according to Steele, it's an aesthetic that embraces the many moods and meanings of black: death, defiance, devilry, and dandyism. Victorian mourning gowns of mauve are gothic; so too are memento mori such as skulls and skeletons.

In gothic fashion, black is more than black—it's blackness itself, the dark side embodied in a single, sombre shade. And it's flattering—who doesn't look good in it? Steele believes that gothic fashion is able to embody the essence of death because fashion and death are cut from the same cloth. Fashion, she says, is a form of death, an artful, artificial form: it is constantly dying so that it can come back in a new silhouette, a new shape, a new style. All fashion is undead. All fashion is a Frankenstein monster.

"The uncanny is 'nothing new,'" Steele says, quoting Sigmund Freud, "but on the contrary, 'something which is familiar,' which has been 'repressed,' and which recurs.'"

If the uncanny recurs, then the gothic is the uncanniest fashion of all. The first goth was Satan – the Dark One, the Prince of Darkness.

"Throughout world history," Steele writes, "black has been associated with night and darkness, and, by extension, with death, danger and evil." She notes that until the 19th century, black dye was dear. Only the wealthy were able to buy black cloth. Black was the colour of Beelzebub, and of nobility.

Byron wore black. Black perfectly captured the poet's reputation as a libertine and a rebel. Baudelaire wore black. It was said that he resembled "Byron dressed by Beau Brummell." Byron was a Romantic poet; Brummell an English dandy who revolutionized the cut of menswear in the early 19th century. Baudelaire was a bit of both: a red-blooded rebel who comported himself with an air of indifference, of *froideur*.

Birds of a feather: Byron, Baudelaire, Beau Brummell—and Siouxsie Sioux? "The most important contemporary manifestation of the gothic is the goth subculture," asserts Steele, "which developed in the late 1970s." Siouxsie Sioux started out as a punk, an acolyte of the Sex Pistols. She wore bondage gear and PVC. After 1976, when she started singing with her own band, The Banshees, she developed a more macabre, mysterious look. She mixed and matched pieces of vintage Vivienne Westwood with vintage Victoriana. With her pale, powdered face, she resembled a character from *The Cabinet of Dr. Caligari*; with her black-rimmed eyes, she resembled Alla Nazimova, the lascivious vamp of silent movies.

Along with a few other figures from the post-punk scene—Peter Murphy of the band Bauhaus, Ollie Wisdom of the band Specimen, which established the Batcave club in London—Siouxsie created the classic goth costume. It caught on with disaffected kids across the world, loners and losers who longed to be poets and rebels and disinterested dandies. It was codified as completely as Victorian mourning had been. In 1884, a widow in deep mourning could only wear black crepe; after a year and a half, purple became acceptable. In 1984, a goth's hair had to be dyed bottle blond or blue-black. Fishnet stockings for girls; skirts for girls and guys. Black was non-negotiable. Goths seemed to be grieving, but for whom? For what?

Siouxsie's look lives on. It has lasted longer and made more of an impact than any look Madonna or David Bowie dreamed up. It won't die. In malls across America, stores peddle the silhouettes she donned decades ago. It's rising up in new and novel ways: cyber goths wear reflective fabrics; vampire goths wear fangs; gravers are goths who incorporate the electric colours of ravers into their ensembles. The steam punk style combines the lace and corsetry of the Victorian goth with the goggles and gas masks of the industrial goth. Steele sees strains of goth in punk fashion, death metal fashion, psychobilly and rockabilly fashion.

Why does goth fashion never die? Steele says it can't. To her, all fashion is an uncanny recurrence, a gothic phantasmagoria. Which raises the question: if all fashion is goth, then can't all clothes—bridal wear, cruise wear, sportswear—be considered goth fashion? The book is haunted by this possibility, though the truth is: goth has its own glamour, its own gloss, its own sangfroid, not because it shows death in the form of fashion, but rather because it shows that *death is a form of fashion*.

It's the last word.

2008/2021

ACKNOWLEDGEMENTS

Thanks to Micah Adams, Abbas Akhavan, Howard Akler, David Altmejd, Guy Anderson, Nathalie Atkinson, Dodie Bellamy, Alex Bierk, Peter Birkemoe, Kyle Buckley, Tony Burgess, Scott Cataffa, Joey Comeau, Dennis Cooper, Trinie Dalton, Kim Dorland, Hedi El Kholti, Vincent Fecteau, Claire Foster, Robert Glück, Susan Grimbly, James Gunn, Bruce Hainley, Richard Hawkins, Sheila Heti, William E. Jones, Susan Kernohan, David Keyes, Jennifer Krasinski, Micah Lexier, Jack McBride, Jason McBride, Melissa McCormack, Casey McKinney, Don McLeod, Serah-Marie McMahon, Michael Maranda, Alex Molotkow, Donal Mosher, Philip Monk, Paul P, Michael Palmieri, Christopher Paulin, Ian Pearson, Kevin Perry, Ian Phillips, Charlie Porter, Joanne Saul, Lori Seymour, Ken Sparling, Matthew Stadler, Al Stencell, Shirley Stencell, Adam Sternbergh, Liz Sullivan, Conan Tobias, Scott Treleaven, David Velasco, Samara Walbohm, Christopher Waters, Greg Wells, Edmund White, Deborah Wilton, Alana Wilcox, Marco Zanini.

Special thanks to Richard Porter and Pilot Press, and to Trust Judy Blame.

In memoriam: Judy Blame, Kevin Killian, David Livingstone and my Mom and Dad, Cynthia and Murray McCormack.